Designing Gardens with Flora of the American East

Designing Gardens with Flora of the American East

CAROLYN SUMMERS

RUTGERS UNIVERSITY PRESS

NEW BRUNSWICK, NEW JERSEY, AND LONDON

Library of Congress Cataloging-in-Publication Data

Summers, Carolyn, 1954–

Designing gardens with flora of the American East / Carolyn Summers.

p. cm.

Includes bibliographical references and index.

ISBN 978–0–8135–4706–0 (hardcover : alk. paper)

ISBN 978–0–8135–4707–7 (pbk. : alk. paper)

1. Landscape gardening—East (U.S.) 2. Endemic plants—East (U.S.)

3. Gardening to attract wildlife—East (U.S.) 4. Biodiversity conservation—East (U.S.)

5. Native plant gardening—East (U.S.) I. Title.

SB473.S8546 2010

712.0974—dc22

2009016197

A British Cataloging-in-Publication record for this book
is available from the British Library.

Visit our Web site: http://rutgerspress.rutgers.edu

Manufactured in the United States of America

TEXT DESIGN AND COMPOSITION BY JENNY DOSSIN

For Katy and David

CONTENTS

PREFACE

As a child, I was more interested in animals than gardens. I could be coaxed into helping my mother harvest vegetables and fruits, especially strawberries, but no one had to cajole me into rescuing chipmunks from cats or nursing baby raccoons. As a young adult, I discovered groups, for example, the Fund for Animals and the Humane Society of the United States, who lobbied for the welfare of animals. As I educated myself, however, I began to focus on a key issue that these groups could not grapple with: habitat destruction. Other groups, like the Audubon Society, the Nature Conservancy, the Trust for Public Land, and the Natural Resources Defense Council, confronted the habitat issue more directly, either through habitat purchase and preservation or by a combination of political persuasion and legal tactics. Despite my admiration for this work, I chose landscape architecture over law school.

My goal was simple: I would learn how to make human-dominated landscapes accommodate the needs of wildlife. As the field of landscape architecture is allied closely with engineering and architecture, professions that have caused a tremendous amount of wildlife habitat destruction, I approached my education with a healthy dose of skepticism. Early on, however, I was fortunate to read *Design with Nature* by Ian McHarg, probably the first book to thoroughly set forth principles of ecological design, and to learn about the ongoing work of Andropogon Associates, a Pennsylvania-based landscape architecture firm, and its promotion of the use of indigenous plants for commercial and residential landscapes. Andropogon was influential for two reasons: it was the first commercial firm I had heard of that was doing the work I dreamed of doing, and, through its work, I began to understand the importance of indigenous plants in the landscape.

As I studied indigenous plants, a strange thing happened. The plants grew on me. I began to love the plants themselves for their own unique qualities, quite apart from their usefulness in providing food and shelter for wildlife. My definition of wildlife broadened to include the myriad species of wild flora: strangely beautiful orchids, delicate spring ephemerals such as trout lily, robust yet vulnerable meadow lilies, and resilient oak trees. Similarly, my definition of wildlife habitat expanded to include special areas, such as bogs, that support specialized plant communities with only a limited number of animal species. Happily, as it turns out, if you support wild flora, you support all wildlife.

Through this book, I hope to share much of what I have learned about our lovely, unique, indigenous plants. I also hope to enlist other gardeners and professional landscapers in the creation of beautiful, healthy, productive gardens that are not exclusively for human use, but will also nurture and enhance, instead of obliterating, wildlife habitat. Our wild heritage is vanishing at an alarming rate. Learning to know and grow indigenous plants is one way we gardeners can begin repairing the frayed fabric of our landscape right in our own back yards. Research, in particular the work of entomologist Douglas Tallamy summarized in his recent book, *Bringing Nature Home*, demonstrates that indigenous plants are the best sources of food and shelter for our wildlife. In addition to wildlife benefits, I encourage gardeners to widen their scope and see for themselves the versatility and aesthetic benefits of our wild floral heritage.

During the process of my research for this book, however, I became convinced that I, too, needed to widen my scope. Many of our fruits and vegetables come from other continents. Some nonindigenous plants that have been in use here for perhaps two or three hundred years have caused no obvious problems (as far as we have yet learned), aside from displacing natural vegetation. Others have become horribly, expensively invasive and now run rampant, smothering acres of natural vegetation and threatening rare indigenous plants with extinction. Worse still are those that may carry nonindigenous insects and fungal or other pathogens that threaten whole populations of important plant species.

Clearly, nonindigenous plants for food and landscaping are here to stay. Responsible gardeners need information to be able to choose the most useful, least harmful ones. And so the scope of this book widened from a discussion of the many ways to use indigenous plants in the garden to include the facts gardeners require to make informed choices about when, where, and how to use nonindigenous species with the least amount of harm to the regional landscape surrounding their gardens. This book catalogs nonindigenous species that have been in use since the colonial period without naturalizing, as well as ways to minimize risks from newer imports. A list of plants known to be highly invasive is provided, so that gardeners may avoid them altogether. None of the plant lists in this book are meant to be exclusive; when choosing among many candidates, I was forced, for the sake of brevity, to forgo including many good and useful plants.

As suburbia moves inexorably outward, and more and more "vacant land" becomes subdivided, the fate of our remaining wild nature (both plants and animals) will depend on the mainstream use of indigenous plants in human-dominated landscapes. That may seem improbable to readers currently living in more pristine rural areas. No one who lives in or near an eastern city, however, and pays attention to roadside vegetation patterns, can possibly miss the trend. As we drive from more rural areas toward the inner cities, the roadside vegetation goes from recognizable, functioning plant communities to unattractive jumbles of exotic plants, such as mugwort, Norway maple, and Oriental bittersweet vine (all escaped from gardens), that have completely crowded out indigenous plant life. We gardeners, you see, have more power than we know.

Mainstream awareness of indigenous plants for gardening is rising, but if recent magazine articles are any indication, it is hardly pervasive. I reviewed the summer 2008 issues of four prominent gardening periodicals and the results were not terribly encouraging. In three of the four, more than three-quarters of the articles dealt exclusively with exotic, nonindigenous plants. Most garden design plans did not include even one single species native to North America. The fourth, *Fine Gardening*, was a pleasant surprise, with close to half of the articles including the use of indigenous plants, notably an article on summer-blooming shrubs; fourteen of the twenty-eight plants mentioned were indigenous. This is progress.

In analyzing these and other publications, it occurred to me that one of the biggest hurdles to mainstream use of indigenous plants (aside from the nursery industry itself) is a general confusion between design and science, style and substance, horticulture and ecology. Many gardeners are simply confusing the substance of indigenous plants with the style of naturalistic gardening. In a sad case of unintentional irony, a book specifically about English cottage gardens for American gardeners featured only fourteen indigenous perennials out of seventy-six. Many cottage gardens located in England contain a higher percentage of American plants than that. In fact, one could design an entire garden in the mode of Versailles using plants indigenous to eastern North America, and no one but a botanist would ever guess. As it happens, the July 9, 2008, edition of the *Washington Post* featured an article about Alain Baraton, the head gardener at Versailles, who is currently engaged in, among other sustainable initiatives, replacing those plants that are not native to Europe with indigenous European plants. While I have not undertaken anything as ambitious, this book does include a list of indigenous plants well-suited for formal gardens and other specific applications, together with design sketches that illustrate how to make simple substitutions of indigenous for nonindigenous plants, retaining a traditional look without any change in design.

Overall trends, fortunately, favor increased use of indigenous plants, including sustainability initiatives similar to green building standards. The Sustainable Sites Initiative, for example, a partnership among the American Society of Landscape Architects, the Lady Bird Johnson Wildflower Center, the United States Botanic Garden, and other stakeholder organizations, is developing and promoting the Standards and Guidelines for Sustainable Sites (http://www.sustainablesites.org/report). In another sign of progress, in May 2008, the New York Botanical Garden received a $15 million gift from the Leon Levy Foundation to create a new 3.5-acre native plant garden. In 2001, Westchester County (New York) Executive Andrew Spano signed executive order no. 1, requiring all Westchester County properties to use only plants indigenous to the county, whenever possible.

This book is intended to help gardeners, designers, and landscapers ease the transition from mostly nonindigenous to mostly indigenous landscapes. This may require busting a few myths along the way and the introduction of a few gorgeous, but seriously underutilized plants. Although the design and ecological concepts discussed here are applicable to most areas, the advice regarding specific plants is limited to the Northeast. As defined in the standard reference *Manual of Vascular Plants of Northeastern United States and Adjacent Canada*, by Henry A. Gleason and Arthur Cronquist (commonly known as *Gleason and Cronquist's Manual*), this region includes the New England and Middle Atlantic states as far south as Virginia and Kentucky, west to Indiana, the northern portion of Missouri, Iowa, and Minnesota, bounded on the north by Canada.

Even if this book fails to inspire the highest levels of landscape creativity, it will have succeeded in its mission if some of the more mundane design sketches become templates for the mainstream use of indigenous plants. Personally, I have no problem with landscapes that conform outwardly to social norms. Let's take it one step further and make sure our plants conform—biologically—with our natural surroundings. As we have already seen, gardeners quite literally hold the power to remake the world. Let's see if we can put it back together again.

ACKNOWLEDGMENTS

From my parents, I received two wonderful gifts: from my mother, the gift of gardening; from my father, the gift of writing. Without those gifts, this book could not have been written. Another precious contribution, the gift of time, came from my husband and my daughter. Thank you, David and Katy, for your love and patient support. I would also like to thank David for the gift of a digital camera; all of the photographs used in this book are my own.

I want to thank Albert F. Appleton, former commissioner of the New York City Department of Environmental Protection, my mentor and former boss, for on-the-job training and the gift of empowerment. Through his visionary leadership, we were able to implement the first indigenous plant policy in the City of New York. To this day, in one of the densest urban centers in the world, all of the department's construction contracts that include landscaping specifications require the use of indigenous plants, including those for construction in the city's upstate watersheds.

Finally, this book would never have been written had it not been commissioned by my dear friend, Michele Hertz. Actually, "commissioned" is not accurate; badgered is really what she did, for several years, until I finally finished. I returned the favor; the lovely drawings in this book are hers. Thank you, Michele, for the gift of friendship.

LIST OF ABBREVIATIONS

cv. . . . . cultivar (singular)

cvs. . . . . cultivars (plural)

sp. . . . . species (singular)

spp. . . . . species (plural)

subsp. . . . . subspecies (singular)

subspp. . . . . subspecies (plural)

var. . . . . variety

vars. . . . . varieties

Designing Gardens with Flora of the American East

1

WHY

SHOULD WE

GARDEN

WITH

INDIGENOUS PLANTS?

After 1492, the world's ecosystems
collided and mixed as European vessels
carried thousands of species to new homes
across the oceans. . . . It is arguably the
most important event in the history of
life since the death of the dinosaurs.

....

CHARLES C. MANN, "America, Found and Lost"

We gardeners are a hopeful, well-intentioned lot, digging in to spread beauty and fruitful bounty far and wide. Many of us plant trees that we can never hope to see at maturity, yet we carry on, serene in the knowledge that we are enhancing the landscape for future generations. For most of us, the landscapes we tend are constrained by the invisible property lines that define our personal residences. Rarely do we have the opportunity to consider the individual and collective effects of our gardens on the larger landscape. While no gardener or landscape professional would ever intentionally harm the environment, no garden is an island. Even the best landscape professionals make mistakes that can have far-reaching, lasting, negative consequences. When Frederick Law Olmsted designed New York City's famous Central Park in 1858, he made extensive use of nonindigenous Norway maples (*Acer platanoides*), never guessing that this species would aggressively invade and change surrounding wild forests.

Figure 1.1. Trout lily (*Erythronium americanum*) is one of the ephemeral spring wild-flower species that cannot reproduce under the shade of Norway maples.

More than one hundred years later, scientists studying the spread of Norway maple into regional forests have discovered that this tree's trait of leafing out especially early prevents adequate light from reaching many species of spring wildflowers, making it impossible for them to reproduce (figure 1.1). In addition, there is less food available for baby birds in forests overrun by Norway maples. Baby birds depend on a steady diet of insect larvae (caterpillars) that eat forest tree leaves. Because the leaf chemistry of Norway maples is completely different from that of sugar maples and other indigenous maples (*Acer* spp.), its leaves are unpalatable and cannot be eaten by insect larvae. Unlike the other trees in the forest, Norway maples cannot provide a source of food for either caterpillars or the baby birds that eat them. These and other findings, unfortunately, have had little effect on the nursery industry; the Norway maple remains one of the top-selling trees in America, and unsuspecting gardeners are still planting them in residential landscapes to the detriment of the surrounding forests and their wildlife inhabitants.

Understandably, in the absence of readily available information to the contrary, most gardeners will follow their personal inclinations in choosing the plants most pleasing to the eye (and, occasionally, nose), with the laudable goal of beautifying their surroundings. Experienced gardeners know that they must choose plants that will do well in the soil, moisture, and light available in their backyard, but beyond that, personal and stylistic preferences will most likely dictate plant selection. With the exception of devoted wildflower gardeners, plant origin (indigenous versus nonindigenous) is not even a factor to consider when most gardeners choose plants for the home landscape.

Gradually, as awareness of the many benefits provided by indigenous plants has grown, that dynamic is changing. Perhaps for the first time in the history of gardening, a growing number of scientists, landscape architects, and nursery and other "green-industry" professionals are making the case, based on an accumulation of scientific studies, that plant origin is, in fact, a very important point to consider. Many of these studies were begun as the conservation community awoke to the fact that carefully preserved natural areas were being harmed by invasive nonindigenous plants. As scientists studied the obvious smothering and displacement of natural vegetation caused by the invasives, many more subtle problems, such as disruptions in the food web, emerged. Ultimately, we have learned that because indigenous plants form the foundation of the food chain, only through maintaining the health of our natural plant communities, such as fields and forests, can we maintain our regional landscape and the wildlife that make it their home. That simple fact carries profound implications for the choices we make as gardeners. The remainder of this chapter attempts to explain, in greater detail and as clearly as possible, the reasons why we should use indigenous plants in our gardens. First, though, it is important to define the term *indigenous plant* and discuss why I am using it instead of the similar, more common term *native plant*.

> An indigenous plant is one that evolved over millennia in the same habitat in which it is currently found.

An indigenous plant is one that evolved over thousands of years in the same habitat in which it is currently found. The expressions are often used interchangeably; however, *indigenous* more precisely applies to regional or ecological boundaries, whereas *native* is frequently applied more broadly to political or even continental boundaries, for example, when we speak of the native plants of the United States or of North America. In choosing to use *indigenous* rather than *native* to describe the plants discussed here, I am emphasizing a particular regional boundary, northeastern North America, and the ecological interactions that take place within. Another term, *wildflower*, is ambiguous and may refer to either indigenous or nonindigenous plants. Many common wildflowers often are presumed to be indigenous (table 1.1) but were actually introduced from other continents and have naturalized widely.

The indigenous plants of the Northeast evolved during the advance and retreat of glaciers and before the arrival of European colonists. The Rocky Mountains proved to be a formidable barrier to plant migration; however, the fortunate fact that these mountains range from north to south instead of from east to west allowed for many northeastern plants to migrate south to escape the encroaching glaciers and back north again as the ice receded. Europe was not as lucky; its mountains range from east to west, and this fact has been cited as a possible explanation for the relative impoverishment of the northern European flora as compared with that of northeastern North America.

Recent molecular analyses of plants, combined with scientific studies in paleoecology by researchers such as David Barrington and Catherine Parris at the University of Vermont, have shed some light on the mysteries of plant migrations. Interestingly, some plants were able to find refuge in

---

Table 1.1.

Examples of Nonindigenous Wildflowers Frequently Mistaken for Indigenous Wildflowers

As early as 1672, some of the plants listed below had already naturalized.

Artemisia vulgaris, mugwort

Centaurea stoebe subsp. *micranthos*, spotted knapweed

Cichorium intybus, chicory

Daucus carota, Queen Anne's lace

Galium odoratum, sweet woodruff

Gypsophila elegans, baby's breath

Hemerocallis fulva, daylily

Hesperis matronalis, dame's rocket

Leucanthemum vulgare, daisy

Rosa multiflora, multiflora rose

Stellaria media, chickweed

Taraxacum officinale, dandelion

Thymus vulgaris, thyme

Trifolium pratense, red clover

Tussilago farfara, coltsfoot

Figure 1.2. The carnivorous sundew (*Drosera rotundifolia*), a circumboreal plant, is found in bogs across the Northeast, the Arctic, and parts of Europe.

unglaciated areas of the Arctic, possibly along the Atlantic coast. Similar to the manner in which humans and other mammals spread across continents in the wake of receding glaciers, some plants were also able to migrate, giving rise to the small but interesting class of plants we call *circumpolar* or *circumboreal*. These plants are indigenous to more than one region, even in some cases, to more than one continent. Some circumboreal species have maintained continentwide ranges across the Arctic region, while the ranges of others have become limited to isolated, *relict* populations. Despite the fact that time and space have long separated different populations of these plants, they did not evolve into different species, as would usually be the case. Two common garden plants, harebell, also known as bluebells of Scotland (*Campanula rotundifolia*), and common juniper (*Juniperus communis*), are examples of plants indigenous to both North America and Europe. There are many other circumboreal plants, such as the sundew (figure 1.2); some of the more common ones are listed in appendix A.

Of course, as the plants migrated, so did the wildlife. It is this shared history of migration and evolution that underlies the key role of indigenous plants as the foundation of the food web. Over time and space, as northeastern plants and animals evolved together, they became interdependent in ways we are just beginning to understand. Although not truly symbiotic, these plants and animals work together to meet each other's needs. Indigenous plants are always the best, and, in most cases the only, tolerable source of food for indigenous insects. Many of our butterflies, moths, bees, and other pollinators are *host specific*. In other words, at the larval or caterpillar stage of their life cycle, these insects are utterly dependent on one or two groups of plant species for food. Such plants are referred to as *host plants*. Some caterpillars are limited to just a single species of host plant, for example, those of the Harris's Checkerspot butterfly (*Chlosyne harrisii*), which can eat only a single species of flower, the flat-topped aster (*Aster umbellatus*). Some species of bees may exhibit similar interdependencies. In *The Forgotten Pollinators*, Stephen Buchmann and Gary Nabhan describe the dwarf bearclaw poppy, (*Arctomecon humilis*), which can only be pollinated by one dedicated species of pollinator, in this case, a lone species of bee, *Perdita meconis*. Without pollination, the poppy's seeds remain sterile, and it cannot reproduce. Not surprisingly, the dwarf bearclaw poppy is on the federal endangered species list.

> Indigenous plants form the foundation of the food chain and, therefore, maintain our regional landscape and the wildlife that make it their home.

Let's look at how these interdependent insects and plants contribute to the food web in a healthy, northeastern deciduous forest (figure 1.3). The seasonal cycle of plant growth, flowering (reproduction), and dormancy, with the accompanying migrations and awakenings of birds, butterflies, and other animals of the region, is one of the earth's most unique and splendid pageants. While trees are still bare, spring sunlight wakens the spring ephemerals, flowers that transform and carpet the forest floor. In a burst of activity, they complete their reproductive cycle before trees have even finished leafing out. These first flowers of spring attract and provide nectar for newly aroused flies and bees and other insects. Soon the migratory birds come to nest and reproduce, many of them dependent on the insects that feed on the abundant flowers. As the leaves gradually unfold, caterpillars and other insect larvae are coming out of winter shelter to feast, just in time to provide food for newly hatched baby birds. In autumn, the reproductive cycle comes, literally, to fruition, as migrating birds devour the abundant berries produced by trees, shrubs, and vines of the forest, spreading seeds far and wide. The timing of these myriad events—flowering, leafing out, fruiting, feeding, and nesting—is exquisitely synchronized in a complex dance, worked out over millennia.

These healthy ecological processes are self-perpetuating in the absence

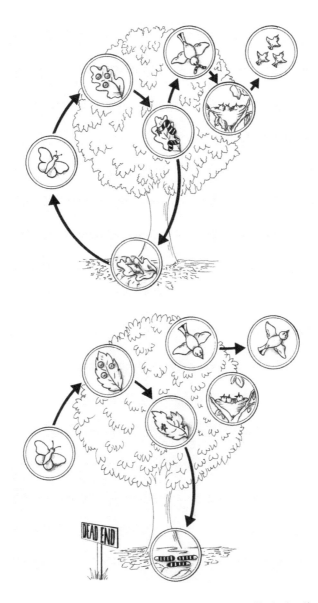

Figure 1.3. Birds and butterflies: a food web. The first scene illustrates the relationship among indigenous plants, insects, and birds. The female butterfly lays her eggs on the indigenous tree. Caterpillars hatch and thrive on the indigenous leaves. The mother bird feeds some of the caterpillars to her nestlings; the other caterpillars form chrysalises before turning into adult butterflies. In the second scene, a female butterfly mistakenly lays her eggs on a nonindigenous tree, and the web is broken. Caterpillars hatch and cannot eat; the mother bird loses a ready supply of food and must search longer and harder to feed her young. Illustration by Michele Hertz.

of, and sometimes in spite of, human influence. Northeastern plant communities are adapted to natural disturbances such as storms, fire, or drought, which may delay or temporarily suspend some processes, but rarely cause long-term damage. Introduction of nonindigenous plants, insects, and blights, on the other hand, disrupts ecological processes on a continuous basis long after the initial disturbance, as these biological organisms have their own self-perpetuating mechanisms, much as cancer behaves in the human body. While our fields and forests appear outwardly resilient, even impenetrable, a silent struggle for survival is taking place everywhere (figure 1.4). When indigenous plants compete with each other, the playing field is level, and a balance is usually struck. Nonindigenous species, on the other hand, have a few distinct competitive advantages.

The most successful nonindigenous invaders exhibit reproductive traits that allow rapid colonization of disturbed areas. For example, many of them produce an overabundance of seeds and can eventually overwhelm indigenous seed sources. Some are evergreen and benefit from year-round access to the sun's energy. Even deciduous ones are genetically programmed to wake

....

Garlic mustard (*Alliaria petiolata*) is a nonindigenous invasive herb that physically displaces other wildflowers in the ground layer of closed-canopy forests. A member of the mustard family, this plant fools butterflies into thinking that it is a host plant. When butterflies that use indigenous mustards as host plants lay eggs on garlic mustard, the newly hatched caterpillars cannot survive. This would be bad enough, but recent research from the Harvard Forest in Petersham, Massachusetts, shows that garlic mustard threatens the forest canopy as well. Over millions of years of evolutionary processes, forests evolved an interdependent relationship with mycorrhizal fungi. As a critical component of most soil food webs, mycorrhizal fungi create vast networks in the organic-rich upper layers and form mutually beneficial relationships with the roots of trees and other plants. The fungi assist the delivery of water and minerals to forest trees and may also protect them from pathogens. Researchers led by Kristina Stinson of Harvard University found that garlic mustard secretes toxic phytochemicals that kill off the fungi and prevent it from colonizing tree roots. Cut off from the services provided by the fungal networks, forests will inevitably decline. Weeding out garlic mustard is important not only to make space for delicate wildflowers and to protect butterflies but also to keep the entire forest from being slowly poisoned.

....

Figure 1.4. In boa constrictor–fashion, this Oriental bittersweet vine (*Celastrus orbiculatus*) wrapped itself around the tree and gradually pulled it to the ground.

up and leaf out earlier in spring, giving them a reproductive head start. They are forever "out of sync," physically displacing indigenous vegetation and disrupting natural processes. The main advantage, however, seems to be that because nonindigenous plants and other organisms did not coevolve with our flora and fauna, they enjoy immunity from indigenous pests and diseases. They left behind the pests and diseases that would keep them in check in their place of origin. This phenomenon has been studied since 1859, when it was first proposed by Charles Darwin as the *enemy release hypothesis.*

The rapid pace of human-induced change enhances the ability of invasive plants and other organisms to spread by weakening natural systems, thereby rendering individual elements more vulnerable to invasion and less resilient in the face of introduced pathogens. In times past, natural systems were the dominant forces in the landscape. Even a large fire or hurricane occurred within the natural matrix; damage was contained and surrounded by the intrinsic elements that would repair the damage. With the rise of human-dominated landscapes, the reverse is true. When a bulldozer levels five hundred acres for a shopping mall or opens up a new swale along a roadside, the area devoid of vegetation is like an open wound, and invasive nonindigenous plant seeds act as infectious agents (figure 1.5).

Figure 1.5. One side of this country road has become infested with Japanese knotweed (*Polygonum cuspidatum*); once this plant has a foothold, it will continue to spread aggressively, displacing the surrounding natural vegetation.

This unfortunate trend is already visible in most of the New York metropolitan area, where an inventory by the Brooklyn Botanic Garden shows that five of the fifteen most widespread woody plants are nonindigenous. Many of these plants are capable of spreading without human assistance, in other words, *naturalizing* along roadways to the exclusion of indigenous trees, shrubs, and vines. Forest fragments surrounded by suburban development with accompanying nonindigenous landscapes have had their characteristics profoundly altered by the invasive plants and are no longer recognizable as northeastern hardwood forests. Recently, scientists have come to realize that weedy fragments devoid of most indigenous plant species also lack the lower levels of the animal food chain. These are primarily insects that require indigenous plants to complete their life cycles. Such changed landscapes are largely barren and cannot support more than a fraction of the normal level of biodiversity that a natural forest exhibits. While wildlife is, presumably, the first to feel the effects of surviving in stressed, weakened landscapes, impacts to human health are becoming increasingly obvious. Scientists, including Richard Ostfeld at the Cary Institute for Ecosystem Studies in Millbrook, New York, have found that patterns of suburbanization positively influence the complex life cycle of the spirochete that causes Lyme disease. More recently, researchers led by Scott C.

Williams from the Connecticut Agricultural Experiment Station working with the University of Connecticut are actually recommending the removal of the nonindigenous shrub Japanese barberry (*Berberis thunbergii*), which they have found to harbor abnormally high levels of Lyme-infected ticks. Unfortunately, the task of removing barberries and other invasives often falls to farmers, foresters, and conservation professionals rather than the nursery industry that perpetuates and profits from them. Annual costs for maintaining farms, forests, and preserves relatively free from invasives are estimated in the billions of dollars. This is obviously a poor allocation of scarce financial resources, particularly for the nonprofit conservation community. Even in ordinary garden use, nonindigenous plants require extra resources in terms of fertilizer and water as compared with their indigenous counterparts. Lawns are especially resource-intensive.

If some of this information is leading you to think about which indigenous plants you could add to your garden, then this book is on the right track. The research upon which it is based directs gardeners to concentrate on using the plants of the region in which their garden is located. Within that advice, there is ample room for interpretation, not to mention trial and error. As global warming sets in, plant hardiness zones are becoming a moving target. Regional boundaries are not rigidly defined, and plants do move around. My work in New York State has provided me with knowledge of the indigenous plants of the Northeast, as broadly defined in *Gleason and Cronquist's Manual*, and the plant lists and other advice that I offer are appropriate for this region. The following chapters explain the consequences of plant selection to help gardeners make the most responsible choices, but, in the end, gardeners must decide for themselves which plants to include and which to exclude.

Use indigenous plants for the following purposes:

✓ To conserve resources and reduce maintenance
✓ To maintain a healthy web of life
✓ To maintain natural processes in our forests, wetlands, fields, and meadows
✓ To maintain the ability of indigenous plants to reproduce
✓ To preserve our regional aesthetic identity and sense of place
✓ To prevent new infestations of invasive plants and disease
✓ To provide the best—often the only—available food and habitat for wildlife

---

In writing this, it is not my expectation that the reader will run right out and start digging up and discarding mature specimens of Japanese andromeda (*Pieris japonica*) and other nonindigenous plants. (If, on the other hand, you are bored with the old plantings, this book may provide the perfect excuse.) Unless you are the rare individual who purchased a home in a new subdivision from a developer who went bankrupt prior to the installation of sod, no one gardens on a clean slate. Garden transformations take time. Remember that by adding just a few indigenous plants to your garden, you will make it a more hospitable, recognizable place for local wildlife and you will have taken an important first step toward integrating your garden with its natural surroundings.

2

WILDLIFE

IN

FIELD,

FOREST,

AND GARDEN

If we would have moths and butterflies,
we must first have caterpillars.

....

FRANK C. PELLETT, *Flowers of the Wild*

Many wonderful and entertaining books have been written on the subject of backyard wildlife gardens. Some of my favorites are listed in the bibliography. Here, I try not to duplicate that work but rather give a brief contextual overview of wildlife needs and then some specific examples of how indigenous plants, in particular, best provide for those needs. With a few recent exceptions, that emphasis has been missing from most of the bird and butterfly habitat books that I have reviewed. At the end of the chapter, I offer a few design, maintenance, and planting suggestions. Plants listed are suggestions only; as there are slightly fewer than two thousand species native just to the New York portion of the Northeast, some tough choices had to be made.

All species of wildlife require water, food, and safe hiding/resting/nesting places. We commonly think exclusively of wildlife as animals, yet wildlife can also be defined to include wild *flora*, or plants. Wild flora also have needs. Over thousands of years, plants trained our wildlife to help them reproduce. Wildlife, in turn, taught the plants how to be more efficient producers of their essential needs. This was not, of course, a conscious process;

another name for it is *coevolution*. The result is a deep interdependence among indigenous flora and fauna; scientists and backyard naturalists are slowly unraveling these secrets. The more we discover about these mutual needs, the more we realize the importance of indigenous landscaping for wildlife.

HOSTING BUTTERFLIES

Although many gardeners already are familiar with the concept of host plants for butterfly caterpillars, this fascinating topic is worth a closer look. In the first chapter, I used host specificity as an example of one of the interdependent plant and wildlife relationships that have evolved over time. Perhaps the most familiar examples of host plants are the milkweeds (*Asclepias* spp.), used by the beloved Monarch butterfly (*Danaus plexippus*). Monarch caterpillars must have milkweed plants to eat. If a Monarch mother mistakenly lays her eggs on any plant other than a milkweed, even related ones, such as hemp dogbane (*Apocynum cannabinum*) or the invasive non-indigenous swallowwort vine (*Cynanchum rossicum*), the caterpillars will starve to death. Most of our less charismatic insects are also host specific, limited, for reproductive purposes, to only one plant species or closely related group of species. Research shows that more than 90 percent of our herbivorous insects evolved to tolerate only a few specific plants as food. The reasons behind these relationships have their roots in evolutionary processes. Over time, plants evolved an arsenal of toxic substances within their leaves to protect themselves from being eaten by caterpillars and other insect larvae. As insects perfected the ability to tolerate one or more of these toxic chemicals, they became specialists in consuming the leaves that produced them. No doubt about it, caterpillars are picky eaters. For this reason alone, if you want your garden to be a productive source of butterflies and other pollinators, indigenous plants are essential. The chemical constituents in the leaves of nonindigenous plants are simply too alien for our caterpillars to swallow and digest.

Even closely related indigenous plants may not be interchangeable as host plants. Researchers from Oregon State University chronicled the rediscovery, in the 1990s, of a rare butterfly, Fender's Blue butterfly (*Icaricia icarioides fenderi*), which had not been seen since the 1930s. One of the reasons it had been hard to find was that searchers were combing stands of the common bigleaf lupine (*Lupinus polyphyllus*) as the presumed host plant. The

Figure 2.1. Eastern lupine (*Lupinus perennis*) is the only host plant for the federally endangered Karner Blue butterfly.

butterfly was finally found on three different, much rarer species of lupines, which turned out to be the only true host plants. Here in the Northeast, the federally endangered Karner Blue butterfly, also known as the "Karner" Melissa Blue (*Lycaeides melissa samuelsis*), is dependent on eastern lupine (*Lupinus perennis*), our only indigenous lupine (figure 2.1). The butterfly, however, can be fooled by bigleaf lupine and its hybrids, including the Russell hybrids, which have escaped from eastern gardens and naturalized in many areas. If the butterfly lays her eggs on the bigleaf lupine or its hybrids, the emerging caterpillars will either starve or be poisoned. In the state of Maine, large areas of naturalized bigleaf and hybrid lupines are common, but the Karner Blue butterfly and the eastern lupine can no longer be found. They have been *extirpated* from the state of Maine; in other words, they are locally extinct. Sadly, the citizens of Maine have become so fond of the introduced lupines that control efforts by the National Park Service at Mount Desert Island National Park have met with strong resistance, possibly precluding reintroduction of the endangered butterfly. The attraction to a beautiful flower is understandable and one reason that it is far better to prevent such introductions in the first place.

In contrast to their offspring's faithful attachment to host plants, adult butterflies looking only for a quick sip of nectar are completely promiscuous; indigenous, nonindigenous, annual, perennial, tree, or shrub, anything

Figure 2.2. Dutchman's pipe, or pipevine (*Aristolochia tomentosa*), is one of only three species of pipevines upon which the lovely Pipevine Swallowtail butterfly (*Battus philenor*) can lay her eggs. This photo shows one of the two dozen pipevine caterpillars that ate so much of their host plant that they were forced to climb back down the rain chain.

that flowers and has nectar is fair game. That does not mean, however, that you will want to rush right out and buy the nonindigenous butterfly bush (*Buddleia davidii*). Brought from China by Victorian explorers, butterfly bushes are lanky, deciduous shrubs with arching branches tipped by elongated flowering clusters strongly reminiscent of lilacs. Their showy flowers are, indeed, butterfly magnets, unfortunately, they have become invasive in many areas and they are not used as host plants by any of the butterflies they attract. Many butterfly species live very short lives, on average only about two weeks, and those that do not migrate or winter-over stick close to their home grounds. For this reason, it is important to provide both food and host plants in reasonably close proximity, so that butterflies do not waste precious time. Females may linger too long sipping nectar from a garden full of nonindigenous plants. By the time a butterfly begins to search for a host plant on which to lay her eggs, she may miss the brief window of opportunity offered by her limited life span. Especially if the particular host plant needed is not commonly found in gardens, the butterfly may need to search far and wide until she finds one. If she fails to find a host plant for her eggs, she may lay her eggs on the wrong plant, or she may not lay them at all.

When searching for host plants on which to lay eggs, females are guided by their vision, their sense of smell, and their legs, which have special taste sensors. Despite these aids, a mother butterfly may be fooled into laying her eggs on a nonindigenous plant closely related to her host plant; in all likelihood, the caterpillars will starve or die from poisoning. For example, Pipevine Swallowtail butterflies (*Battus philenor*) are so named because they depend on indigenous pipevine plants (*Aristolochia* spp.) as host plants. An observant butterfly gardener in Florida documented Pipevine Swallowtail caterpillars (figure 2.2) trying to survive on nonindigenous pipevines, noting that after a while they stopped growing and died. This same gardener observed eggs of another butterfly, the Long-Tailed Skipper, on her pipevine plant; the Skipper's caterpillars will not survive on any pipevines. Possibly, mistakes by female butterflies are becoming more frequent as we develop more and more of the landscape, making it harder for all animals, not just butterflies, to find the indigenous plants they need.

HOSTING BEES AND MOTHS

Unlike the indiscriminate nectaring habits of butterflies, many northeastern bees, beetles, and moths join caterpillars in the picky-eater category. As reported in Shepard et al.'s *Pollinator Conservation Handbook*, researchers at the University of California led by Gordon Frankie found that indigenous bees are four times more likely to take nectar and pollen from indigenous plants than from nonindigenous plants. While bees single-mindedly pursue their own needs, they are oblivious to the fact that they are meeting the reproductive needs of the plants by accidentally spreading pollen from one flower to another. The bees are *pollinating* the plants; pollination is one of the best examples of a mutually beneficial wildlife–plant relationship (figure 2.3). Some of our favorite indigenous garden plants, for example, the eastern redbud (*Cercis canadensis*) and blue lobelia (*Lobelia syphilitica*), are pollinated by bumblebees.

Just as some butterflies are dependent on a single host plant, some bees can use the pollen of only one plant to meet their needs; these bees are called *monolectic*. For example, the sunflower bee (*Diadasia enavata*) collects pollen exclusively from sunflowers (*Helianthus annuus*), although the bee is forced to share the pollen with many other species of bees that flock to the pollen-rich flower. *Oligolectic* bees limit their pollen gathering to small groups of related plants, whereas many other bees are generalists, or *polylectic*, indis-

Figure 2.3. These bumblebees (*Bombus* sp.), like other indigenous bees, are four times more likely to take nectar and pollen from indigenous plants than from non-indigenous ones.

Figure 2.4. The earliest blooming ephemerals, like this wood anemone (*Anemone quinquefolia*), provide critical nectar supplies at a time when food is scarce.

criminately gathering pollen wherever they can. Researchers, including entomologist Robert L. Minckley, have found that the creosote bush (*Larrea tridentata*) of the American Southwest may hold the record for attracting the most species of oligolectic bees: twenty-one species, at least some of which may actually be monolectic, using creosote as their sole source of pollen. Monolectic and oligolectic bees must time their emergence to coincide with the flowering of their indigenous host plants and may only be active for a small period of time each year. With the honeybee (a non-indigenous species) in precipitous decline, it is more important than ever to maintain populations of wild indigenous bees and other pollinators.

One of the best ways to maintain pollinators is to preserve indigenous plant species. Northeastern woodland flowers, such as the spring ephemerals and other early bloomers, are critical food supplies for bees and other insects at a time when field and meadow flowers have barely poked their shoots above ground (figure 2.4). Studies comparing pollinator populations at different types of farming operations routinely recommend linking farms to sources of natural vegetation as a means of attracting indigenous pollinators to a farmer's own fruit and vegetable flowers. A study in high alpine meadows in Utah found a link between the loss of certain indigenous meadow flowers and local extirpations of bumblebees. The author of the study, Michael Bowers at the University of Arizona, concluded that it was the loss of the wildflowers, rather than competition between different species of bees, that caused the disappearance of particular bumblebees. Some examples of indigenous plants known to attract bees are listed in table 2.1.

Perhaps most dependent of all on indigenous host plants are the Giant Silk moths, the Lunas, Cecropias, and others (Saturniinae), the Northeast's

Table 2.1.

Plants That Attract Bees

Arctostaphylos uva-ursi, bearberry	*Phacelia* spp., blue curls
Asclepias spp., milkweeds	*Prunus* spp., cherries, plums
Aster spp., asters	*Pycnanthemum* spp., mountain mints
Coreopsis spp., tickseeds	*Rhus* spp., sumacs
Erigeron spp., daisy fleabane	*Rubus* spp., brambles
Helianthus spp., sunflowers	*Senecio* spp., golden groundsels
Penstemon spp., beardtongues	*Vaccinium* spp., blueberries

Figure 2.5. Cocoons of the ethereal Luna moth (*Actias luna*) fall from their host trees in autumn and spend the winter in the leaf litter. For this reason, exporting leaves to the landfill can be a destructive practice.

most spectacular flying insects. These moths are designed only for reproduction; they have no mouths and never feed. Silk moths cannot be lured with any nectar plants, indigenous or nonindigenous. They live for only a few days. The caterpillars of our Silk moths can only tolerate indigenous plants

Table 2.2.
Silk Moth Host Plants

Acer spp., maples	*Lindera benzoin*, spicebush
Alnus spp., alders	*Liquidambar styraciflua*, sweetgum
Betula spp., birches	*Liriodendron tulipifera*, tulip tree
Carya spp., hickories	*Magnolia virginiana*, sweet bay
Cephalanthus occidentalis, buttonbush	*Nyssa sylvatica*, tupelo
Cornus spp., dogwoods	*Populus* spp., aspens
Diospyros virginiana, persimmon	*Prunus* spp., cherries
Fraxinus spp., ashes	*Quercus* spp., oaks
Halesia spp., silverbells	*Salix* spp., willows
Juglans nigra, black walnut	*Sassafras albidum*, sassafras
Larix laricina, larch	*Ulmus* spp., elms

as food, specifically, the leaves of many species of forest trees, such as those listed in table 2.2. In fall, most Silk moths attach their cocoons to leaves on the host tree, but cocoons of the ethereal Luna moth (*Actias luna*, figure 2.5), in particular, fall to the ground and spend the winter in the leaf litter.

BRINGING UP BIRDS

In the past, most ecologists studied natural processes in areas unchanged, or only slightly changed, by humans. One of the best examples is the body of work conducted at the Hubbard Brook Experimental Forest in New Hampshire's White Mountain National Forest, which has produced one of the longest, most continuous databases on the biology, hydrology, geology, and chemistry of forested watersheds. These studies provide valuable information on how natural processes regulate our systems in the absence of direct human influence. More recently, as scientists have learned how quickly and completely human influences are permeating the world, some ecologists have shifted their attention to less pristine areas, including our own suburban gardens. Both approaches have produced studies linking birds and indigenous plants.

Biologists have long discussed which of various factors might control the numbers of birds in a given area. In 2003, researchers led by Jason Jones at Dartmouth College in New Hampshire analyzed fifteen years of ecological data from the Hubbard Brook Experimental Forest. This study, as well as others, have concluded that the numbers of birds are most likely controlled by the availability of food, in the form of insects and other arthropods, needed to feed their babies during the nesting season. In his book *Bringing Nature Home*, Douglas Tallamy shares years of research documenting the key points that more than 96 percent of baby birds require insect larvae as food, while more than 90 percent of those same insect larvae require the leaves or other parts of indigenous plants as food. Taking these findings together illuminates the strands in the food web linking producer to consumer. Butterflies, moths, and other insects lay eggs on indigenous plants; eggs hatch and caterpillars consume the leaves; songbirds find the caterpillars and other insect larvae and feed them to their nestlings, while at the same time improving the health of the surrounding forest by saving the trees and other plants from defoliation (see figure 1.3).

Without indigenous flora for insects to feed on, the food web begins to

Figure 2.6. These baby birds were completely camouflaged along with their nest in thick grasses at the base of a small steeplebush (*Spiraea tomentosa*).

unravel. In practical terms, that means that if our gardens are surrounded by woodlots full of invasive Norway maples, trees-of-heaven (*Ailanthus altissima*), and Bradford pears (*Pyrus calleryana*), and we wish to attract an abundance of birds, we may need to do more than put up bird feeders and nest boxes. We may need to restore the food web by planting indigenous trees and, where feasible, taking down the nonindigenous invasive trees. It also means tolerating a certain amount of leaf damage from insects without resorting to pesticides. The insects that are eating your leaves may be the very food that will attract the birds you want.

Although nesting sites may be secondary in importance to food supply, if nesting sites are unavailable or substandard, the result will be fewer fledglings (figure 2.6). Separate studies conducted by avian ecologists Kathi Borgmann and Amanda Rodewald at Ohio State University, and Dr. Kenneth A. Schmidt at the Cary Institute for Ecosystem Studies, directly compared the reproductive success of birds nesting in indigenous shrubs versus the nonindigenous shrubs multiflora rose (*Rosa multiflora*), European buckthorn (*Rhamnus cathartica*), and Amur honeysuckle (*Lonicera mackii*). Their studies confirmed that more baby birds were lost to predators in nests located within the nonindigenous shrubs. One possible reason put forward by the researchers to explain the result is that the nonindigenous shrubs have wider, but lower, overall shape and their branching structure may allow for greater accessibility by predators. Another contributing factor may stem from the fact that these invasive species form large, homogeneous patches. The lack of variety in their branching structure forces birds to place their nests in a regular pattern that may make it easier for predators to locate them. In contrast, indigenous shrubs and trees used by nesting birds exhibit a much more varied architecture, allowing birds far more options for nest placement.

There is yet another plausible hypothesis, related to palatability, that may contribute to the explanation for these findings. As the leaves of the non-indigenous shrubs in which these nests are located cannot be eaten by insect larvae, there will be no ready source of food for the nestlings. The parent birds may need to forage farther away, leaving the babies alone in the nest for longer periods of time. Birds nesting in the indigenous shrubs will find caterpillars and other insect food close at hand and spend less time away from the nest, offering predators less opportunity for success.

Indigenous hawthorns (trees and shrubs in the genus *Crateagus*) are pre-ferred nesting sites for many species of birds. Most are small trees, but tall enough to discourage many predators; if height does not discourage them, the thorns should. They are densely branching, keeping nests secure in heavy storms. According to Douglas Tallamy's research at the University of Delaware, hawthorns host at least 159 species of butterflies and moths. Birds that value a convenient source of caterpillars will opt to nest in hawthorns. In late winter, year-round residents and early-returning migrant birds will polish off the berries still clinging to hawthorn branches.

Now let's consider how birds prepare for the fall migration. Ornitholo-gists working for the Wildlife Conservation Society at the Bronx Zoo in New York City weighed migratory songbirds that stopped over to fatten up on insects and berries in Bronx Park. Surprisingly, they found that the birds were able to increase their body mass by as much as 20 percent in only a day or two. In storing up energy for their migration, birds require protein from seeds and insects, and nutrients, especially fats (lipids), from berries and other fruits. Comparisons have shown that fruit from nonindigenous plants is less nutritious than fruit from indigenous plants (figure 2.7). Data from research led by Robert A. Johnson from the University of Illinois at Urbana-Champaign shows that there is considerable variation even among indige-nous berries as to which ones have the greatest percentages of the nutritious fats birds need for their long journeys (table 2.3). Berries from the non-

Figure 2.7. Berries of the gray dogwood (*Cornus racemosa*) are extremely nutritious, with high amounts of the fats needed by migrating songbirds. Its leaves are hosts for the Spring Azure butterfly (*Celastrina ladon*).

indigenous shrub Morrow's honeysuckle (*Lonicera morrowii*), found to consist mostly of carbohydrates and water, were dubbed "bird candy" by researcher Jason Love at the University of West Virginia. When given the choice under laboratory conditions, however, birds themselves showed no preference for the more nutritious berries; like humans, birds pick the convenience foods. In any case, berries alone cannot provide enough nutrition, and, in autumn as in spring, insects play a key role in the food web that includes migrating songbirds.

Table 2.3.

Nutritious Berries for Birds (percentage fat content)

Cornus racemosa, gray dogwood (39.9%)
Euonymus atropurpurea, American burningbush (31.2%)
Lindera benzoin, spicebush (33.2%)
Myrica (Morella) pensylvanica, bayberry (50.3%)
Parthenocissus quinquefolia, Virginia creeper (23.6%)
Viburnum dentatum, arrowwood (41.3%)

There is a wealth of fascinating research on birds and their needs, yet there is still much we do not know. More studies are needed, and backyard birders can make valuable contributions. First, however, you must attract them to your backyard. Research to date strongly indicates that an indigenous landscape will host the greatest abundance of birds.

THE AQUATIC FOOD WEB

This chapter emphasizes the ways that indigenous plants sustain wildlife. Although there is a great deal of information on the leaf-eaters and flower-sippers, some of the other strands of the food web have received less attention from the scientific community. This is at least partly the result of the difficulties of studying the more secretive and inaccessible fishes, reptiles, and amphibians. This book would not be complete, however, if I left readers with the impression that the food web begins and ends at the water's edge. Fish foraging in northeastern rivers and streams depend on the organic matter that falls from streamside vegetation. Surprisingly, only during winter do trout rely primarily on aquatic invertebrates for food. During spring, summer, and fall, studies conducted in the Appalachians by researcher Ryan Utz at the University of West Virginia show that trout feed primarily on terrestrial insects, both adults and larvae. Without the indigenous streamside plant community that produces the insects, the trout will have fewer sources of food. The link between healthy trout habitat and natural streamside vegetation has not gone unnoticed by the conservation community. Especially in areas such as New York's Catskills, where trout fishing contributes greatly to local revenues, dedicated citizen volunteers are working with local governments to eradicate stands of invasive Japanese knotweed (*Polygonum cuspidatum*), that prevent natural forest regeneration along prime trout streams.

PRACTICING SCIENCE IN THE GARDEN

Armed with more specific information than ever before regarding the benefits of indigenous plants for wildlife, the next step is to put that knowledge to practical use in our gardens. As is so often the case, however, especially in ecology, more information often leads to more questions. For example, people often ask what color best appeals to butterflies. Because butterflies and humans perceive color in slightly different ways (butterflies are able to see flower patterns in the ultraviolet color range that are invisible to us), perhaps it is better to ask how gardeners can best use color (as we see it) to attract butterflies. Most sources agree, and my own experience confirms, that there is no one single best color; rather, it is the enormity of the color or colors massed against the (usually) green background that draws butterflies and other pollinators from near and far. In a marvelous essay, "What Do Butterflies See?," author Miriam Rothschild writes that butterflies may view the world as a "golden bowl of light."

The design lesson here is to concentrate your butterfly plants in the largest possible grouping; think of a long, wide, perennial border as a butterfly hedge. One compact, carefully planned perennial display can provide nectar all season long. An example is provided in figure 5.16; the possibilities, however, are almost infinite. And now that we know how important it is for female butterflies to lay their eggs on the right host plants, and how difficult it may be for them to find those plants, we can begin to incorporate indigenous host plants into our borders. To simplify the life of female butterflies, as well as gardeners who care for them, a suggested list of perennials that perform double duty, in other words, host plants that also provide nectar, can be found in appendix B.

The finding that butterflies are attracted to colors massed in the landscape ties directly to an important conservation issue. Many people view a field dominated by goldenrods or common milkweed (*Asclepias syriacus*) as an unimportant resource, a *monoculture*, lacking in biodiversity (figure 2.8). But without large concentrations of flowers during times of migration, Monarchs and other migratory butterflies, such as Red Admiral (*Vanessa atalanta*), Painted Lady (*Vanessa cardui*), American Lady (*Vanessa virginiensis*), and Common Buckeye (*Junonia coenia*), might not be able to find adequate nectar sources to fuel their long journey. What may appear monotonous to our eyes must look like heaven to a tired and hungry butterfly. It is probably no accident that the plants known as some of the best sources of nectar for migrating butterflies are often found growing as large showy patches, for example, asters (*Aster* spp.), coneflowers (*Echinacea* spp.), Joe-Pye weed (*Eupatorium* spp.), as well as goldenrod. According to research at the University of Delaware led by Douglas Tallamy, these same plants, all members of the daisy family (Compositae), take first prize in the perennial category for the sheer number of caterpillars they host, between two and three hundred species. Grasses found growing alongside may attract even more caterpillar species (see figure 2.9). Every effort should be made to conserve

Figure 2.8. Although monarchs are the only butterflies that can tolerate milkweed plants, the fluffy Milkweed Tussock moth (*Euchaetes egle*) also thrives on them.

Figure 2.9. The caterpillar of the Virginia Ctenucha moth (*Ctenucha virginica*), along with more than a hundred other species, requires meadow grasses as host plants.

Figure 2.10. A Common Wood Nymph (*Cercyonis pegala*) is enjoying nectar from a large specimen of sparkling white boneset (*Eupatorium perfoliatum*). Contrary to popular belief, butterflies have no trouble finding white-flowered nectar plants.

existing fields, even those that may lack significant floral diversity and, where possible, to create new ones.

Some people mistakenly believe that butterflies are not attracted to white flowers. No one who has seen mountain mints (*Pycnanthemum* spp.), boneset (*Eupatorium perfoliatum*), or the cultivated white-flowered variety of Joe-Pye weed (*Eupatorium maculatum* 'Bartered Bride') mobbed by butterflies will ever make that mistake (figure 2.10). Finding places for white should be no problem; the color white, like the color green, can provide unity in a perennial border of many bright colors. There are also famous gardens dominated by white flowers, known in Victorian times as "moon gardens." White flowers will also attract night-flying moths. By including white and other light-colored flowers in your plantings, you will increase the number of potential visitors and thus the diversity of wildlife in your garden. Suggested nectar plants to attract moths are given in table 2.4.

Not all moths fly at night. Some belong to the select group of day-flying moths, such as the Virginia Ctenucha (*Ctenucha virginica*) and the Hummingbird moths (*Hemaris* spp.). These last are well named, for they often fool people into thinking they are hummingbirds. That is not surprising, because they hover in the same way as hummingbirds over many of the same

Table 2.4.

Nectar Plants for Moths

Asclepias syriacus, common milkweed

Calystegia sepium, hedge false bindweed

Epilobium angustifolium, fireweed

Ipomoea pandurata, wild potato-vine

Lonicera canadensis, American fly honeysuckle

Oenothera biennis, evening primrose

Phlox paniculata, garden phlox

Symphoricarpos albus, snowberry

Trachelospermum difforme, climbing dogbane

tubular-shaped flowers and can even be seen nectaring alongside actual hummingbirds. They are relatively docile, so it is possible to study them closely under sunny skies. Their favorite host plants are indigenous *Viburnum* shrubs, including arrowwood (*V. dentatum*), highbush cranberry (*V. americanum*), nannyberry (*V. lentago*), and wild raisin (*V. nudum*). All of them have showy white flower clusters that can brighten up dark corners of the garden.

Viburnums can also provide the foundation of one of the best landscaping features for migrating and year-round resident birds: a fruiting hedge. By carefully choosing several different species of viburnums and other indigenous shrubs, you can provide almost year-round sustenance. Some of the shrubs will hold their fruit through the winter months, providing food for the permanent residents, as well as the first returning migrants. This is also your opportunity to make it easy for your birds to get plenty of nutrition, by planting more of the shrubs listed in table 2.3. If you have room, adding one or more trees to your hedge, especially evergreens, provides another layer for birds to rest and nest, as well as a place to perch and keep a lookout for predators. A list of indigenous shrubs that provide berries throughout different times of the year is given in appendix C. Many insects will also use the leaves of these shrubs, offering birds a ready source of protein to supplement the carbohydrates and fats of the berries.

In parts of the Northeast, it is not safe to put out year-round bird feeders because of high bear populations. Bears apparently find bird seed to be quite tasty. This is one reason my garden in the Catskills has no bird feeders from spring through fall. Yet, I have plenty of feathered friends keeping

Table 2.5.

Plants That Attract Hummingbirds

Trees and Shrubs

Aesculus glabra, Ohio buckeye

Aesculus pavia, red buckeye

Catalpa spp., catalpas

Ceanothus americanus, New Jersey tea

Clethra alnifolia, sweet pepperbush

Crateagus spp., hawthorns

Liriodendron tulipifera, tulip tree

Rhododendron spp., azaleas and rhododendrons

Vines and Wildflowers

Aquilegia canadensis, wild columbine

Asclepias tuberosa, butterfly milkweed

Bignonia capreolata, crossvine

Campsis radicans, trumpet vine

Lobelia canadensis, cardinal flower

Lobelia syphilitica, blue cardinal flower

Lonicera sempervirens, trumpet honeysuckle

Monarda spp., beebalms

Salvia azurea, blue sage

Spigelia marilandica, Indian pink

me company while they gather caterpillars and other insect larvae for their nestlings. The central garden and the surrounding natural landscape provide an abundance of insects, seeds, berries, and nectar. My resident hummingbird pair do not seem to miss having a bird feeder (and I don't miss cleaning it and keeping it filled). Table 2.5 provides plenty of indigenous plant choices for feeding your hummingbirds naturally.

MAINTAINING WILDLIFE IN YOUR GARDEN

Now that you have carefully chosen and planted butterfly host plants, and the butterflies are flocking to your garden, the responsible gardener must confront an ecological conundrum: Will the garden be a source or a sink? Butterflies provide the simplest example of this concept. If the butterflies you attract complete their life cycle, emerging from their chrysalids in your garden, it has become a *source*, a great and wonderful thing. Butterflies, however, need time to emerge from the chrysalids, and some overwinter in them. Many fall to the ground with the leaves and are well disguised. If you export your leaves to the local landfill every fall, as too many gardeners do, you may very well compost the butterfly chrysalids, thereby turning your garden into what scientists term a *biological sink*. The bottom line: If your garden produces a new generation of butterflies, it is a source. If a butterfly comes to your garden to reproduce and its eggs, caterpillars, or chrysalids are destroyed, your garden is a sink. The good news is that you can provide safe hibernation for butterflies at the same time you lighten your garden workload.

Unfortunately for those who try to maintain a neat garden, myself included, the more untidiness you can tolerate, the better your chances of turning your garden from sink to source for all wildlife, not just butterflies. Keeping your leaves and incorporating them as mulch in your garden is the best way to start. If you have (and want to keep) a lawn, it is necessary to rake the bulk of the leaves off your lawn areas in fall, otherwise they will kill the grass. Other areas, however, need not be disturbed. The cocoons of our lovely Silk moths can be found among the leaf litter underneath their host trees, if one takes the trouble to look while raking, but it is surely simpler not to rake. Letting the leaves lie until spring saves work and improves wildlife habitat.

One difficulty is figuring out when during spring to begin removing the leaves from the tops of perennials and out from underneath trees and shrubs. There is no set date when the butterflies emerge from their chrysalids. Butterflies only fly when the temperature is between 60°F and 80°F, but that temperature range does not necessarily apply to caterpillars. My compromise is to gently rake the leaves in early spring away from the flower beds where ephemerals, such as bloodroot (*Sanguinaria canadensis*) and spring beauties (*Claytonia* spp.), will soon be emerging. As the weather warms, I gradually move the leaves away from the other perennials, as gently as possible, to the far corners of my yard, and pray that I have not made the leaf piles so deep that the butterflies become trapped in their chrysalids, unable to emerge. In early summer, after the caterpillars have emerged and changed (metamorphosed) into butterflies, and before egg-laying begins, I chop the leaves from the previous fall and spread them in the shrub/perennial beds and woodland areas as mulch.

Recently, I have been allowing most of the leaves under shrubs like spice-bush to remain in place without ever raking them out. Unlike oak leaves, which break down slowly, spicebush leaves decompose quickly, and I have learned that the Spicebush Swallowtail is one of those butterfly species that hides its chrysalis among the leaves. My spring workload is less and the chrysalids, if they are there, are safer. By late May, the perennials in front of the spicebushes have grown so that any remnants of last season's spicebush leaves are completely hidden.

Not all butterflies hibernate within a protective chrysalis; some hibernate during other life stages, as an egg, caterpillar, or adult (table 2.6). Hibernating without a chrysalis would seem to be a risky strategy, but many caterpillars find good hiding places, rolling up inside leaves or dried seed pods. The tiny caterpillars of the Common Ringlet (*Coenonympha tullia*) and some Skip-pers overwinter attached to nothing stronger than a blade of grass. Butter-flies that hibernate during winter as adults find shelter under tree bark, in dry stone walls, or tucked away in corners of porches, barns, and other hu-man shelters, not to mention the brush pile you left for the rabbits. Learn-ing about the different hibernation strategies is fun and interesting and will help you adjust your gardening practices for the butterflies' benefit. Recently, I learned that the beautiful orange and black Fritillary butterflies lay their eggs in late summer, when the leaves of their host plants, the violets, are al-ready worn and tattered (figure 2.11). Unperturbed, the female Fritillary de-posits her eggs near the remains of the violet plants. Caterpillars hatch from the eggs and go immediately into hibernation until spring when new vio-let leaves are available. Now that I know, I tiptoe around my violets in late summer and in fall gently sprinkle a few well-crushed leaves as mulch.

....

Table 2.6.

How Butterflies Spend the Winter

Not all butterflies spend the winter in a chrysalis. Some overwinter in other life stages. Examples are given below.

Egg stage: Banded Hairstreak, Bog Copper, Coral Hairstreak
Caterpillar stage: Baltimore, Eastern Tailed Blue, Fritillaries, Pearl Crescent, Viceroy
Chrysalis stage: Silk Moths, Spring Azure, Sulphurs, Swallowtails, Whites
Adult stage: Anglewings, Mourning Cloaks, Tortoiseshells

....

Figure 2.11. The striking orange and black Great Spangled Fritillary (*Speyeria cybele*) lays its eggs near violets, its host plants, in late summer. The caterpillars hatch and immediately hibernate until the next spring, when fresh violet leaves are ready to eat.

Just as creating the garden is a process of learning by doing, so is maintaining it. Let your gardening practices evolve as you observe how the garden is used by both humans and wildlife. My maintenance routine is still far from perfect, but as better information comes my way, and as I learn from my own personal observations, I will adjust my cleanup habits and schedule to be even more protective of my garden's wildlife inhabitants.

UNINVITED GUESTS

Cats

It would be remiss to discuss sources and sinks without tackling the difficult issue of free-ranging cats. Even the most carefully designed wildlife garden can be turned from source to sink by an outdoor cat. I actually know someone who keeps her cats outdoors and has numerous bird houses hung around her garden. There is a serious psychological disconnect at work here, because she has made her garden into an ecological sink. As most of us know, cats will attack and kill small mammals, such as rabbits and chipmunks, as well as reptiles and amphibians, birds, and will even chase and catch large insects, such as butterflies, moths, and dragonflies. It is not their fault; cats, like alligators, just do what comes naturally, if their humans let them. I love cats and for most of my adult life, I have owned cats, usually two at a time. My cats, however, are not ever allowed outside, and they are clean, healthy, and as affectionate and as personable as any dog I have ever known. I raise the last point especially to counter the argument that "cats are not truly happy unless they can go outdoors."

Cats (*Felis sylvestris*) are not indigenous to North America. All domestic cats are descended from Middle Eastern wildcats only a little bigger than our largest house cats. Making itself at home in America, *Felis sylvestris* is estimated to kill hundreds of millions of birds annually. Recognizing a significant threat to wild bird populations, the American Bird Conservancy started Cats Indoors! The Campaign for Safer Birds and Cats. Their Web site provides facts based on actual scientific surveys, examples of which are included here.

In one study, cats wearing bells were found to kill more birds than cats without. Another tested whether well-fed cats still hunt and kill and found that they do. Still another study compared two parks, one without cats and another where cats were being fed. Not surprisingly, the park without cats had twice as many birds. More surprisingly, the park with cats had more than three times as many house mice (an introduced species), and researchers concluded that cats might actually facilitate the expansion of house mice into new areas by reducing the competition from native rodent populations. Researchers at the University of Wisconsin studied rural free-roaming cats and came up with estimates ranging from at least 7.8 million to 217 million birds killed by them annually—just in the state of Wisconsin.

Even at the low end of estimated figures, these mortality rates are clearly unsustainable, and all can be avoided. Your cat will be far healthier, more playful (as you and the catnip ball substitute for prey), and your veterinarian bills will be minuscule. Yes, you will have to change the kitty litter more frequently. This is but a small price to pay for having a garden that is a source, not a sink. The real trick, however, is persuading your friends and neighbors to keep *their* cats indoors. My neighborhood is, at best, a work in progress. Even in rural areas, residents have learned to live with leash laws for their dogs. Maybe a regulatory approach will be required. The wildlife casualty figures cry out for action.

Deer

Human manipulation of deer populations in the northeastern United States is a complete failure. By the late 1800s, we had almost extirpated these lovely creatures. Reintroduced in the early twentieth century in the absence of wild predators, deer have succeeded in becoming dangerous pests in their own right. Hunting by humans is restricted by well-meaning state conservation agencies, encouraged by the less well-intentioned hunting lobby. Regulations that strictly limit the number of does killed function to maintain artificially high deer population levels. Instead of a sustainable number, perhaps ten or twenty deer per square mile, surveys are revealing population densities in the hundreds. Deer are eating themselves out of house and home. In the process, they are leaving little or nothing for other forms of wildlife, including the plants that support all of us.

Data collected by Cornell University's Laboratory of Ornithology indicate that destruction of understory vegetation by deer is making it impossible for Wood Thrushes (*Hylocichla mustelina*) and Black-throated Blue Warblers (*Dendroica caerulescens*) to nest in the forests studied. An editorial in the June 25, 2006, issue of the *New York Times* by Rick Cech, a noted authority on butterflies, listed a series of alarming trends in butterfly populations, even in protected areas, and called for gardeners to grow host plants in their gardens. The case of the disappearing butterflies, of course, is related to the case of the disappearing wildflowers, including host plants; deer browsing was one of the factors mentioned in the editorial. Simple exclosure studies (using fences to keep deer out) consistently have seen wildflower populations bounce back and are proof that deer, not disease, not drought, and not climate change, are causing wildflower declines. Not surprisingly, there is no lack of recent scientific literature, including an excellent overview by Thomas Rawinski of the U.S. Forest Service, documenting the inability of forests to regenerate in the face of unrelenting pressure from deer herds. In a strange twist of fate, some forested parks in New York City continue to maintain healthier understories and wildflower populations than nearby parks in southern Westchester County, no doubt by virtue of their long-term exclusion of deer. The city's deer-free status may not last much longer, however, as deer from New Jersey swim to Staten Island, and Westchester County deer brave the highways and move south into the Bronx.

The most frequent request I receive is for a list of plants that deer will not eat. Experienced gardeners know that such a list is outdated as soon as it is written down. I have seen bulletins from state wildlife agencies less than twenty years old proclaiming that mountain laurel (*Kalmia latifolia*) is toxic to deer. (Perhaps it used to be; this may be an example of evolution in action, as deer, within a few short generations, may have gained the ability to digest laurel toxins.) At this point in time, however, all evergreen foods are survival foods in winter when deer are literally starving. Usually deer do not bother with ground covers, but one winter they came into my front yard, uncovered the snow, and ate my moss phlox (*Phlox subulata*) and bearberry (*Arctostaphylos uva-ursi*). Deer in New Jersey are eating periwinkle (*Vinca* sp.). I used to tell people that deer seemed to leave inkberry (*Ilex glabra*) alone. Not anymore. Especially if it is evergreen, in winter, all bets are off.

A lengthy discussion of a rational deer control policy is clearly outside the scope of this book. It is within its scope, however, to discuss how deer populations affect our ability to garden. Nurseries will occasionally tout nonindigenous plants as being more deer proof than indigenous species. That may have been true ten or twenty years ago, when there were still plenty of wild plants for deer to eat, but more recently, as they have systematically stripped fields and forests bare of everything except grasses and ferns, deer have been forced to acclimate themselves to the full range of our garden plants. Even if the claim that nonindigenous plants are resistant to deer were true (and there is ample proof that it is not), it would be irresponsible to plant more of them and add to the growing problem of barren landscapes. In many circumstances it would actually be better for the environment to plant deerproof trees and flowers made of plastic. At this point, I do not know any serious gardener who will venture to predict what plants a deer will not eat. Soon, it will not be possible to garden at all without deer barriers, either physical or sensory, of some kind. Already, in the New York metropolitan region where I live, this is the prevailing situation.

THE WILD FLORA SANCTUARY

I began this chapter with a definition of wildlife that included wild flora. Quite apart from their importance as the basis of the food web, they are worth preserving and protecting for their beauty and utility alone. According to the Center for Plant Conservation, there are (or were) more than twenty thousand indigenous plant species in the United States. Sadly, more than two hundred of them are now believed to be extinct. Approximately one-quarter, or some five thousand species, is the subject of ongoing conservation efforts. One does not have to look far for the causes of extinction. Many of us are familiar with the direct threat to wildlife posed by widespread conversion of fields and forests to suburban development. Such total and complete habitat loss applies equally to wild plants and is the most irreversible cause of extinction. Another reason is the encroachment by invading nonindigenous plants into natural areas. Unlike outright habitat loss from development, however, if adequate financial resources are made available over long enough periods of time, some of the impacts from invasive species may be reversible.

Deer have become the latest threat. Our wild flora is under increasing pressure from overbrowsing, even in wildlife preserves set aside to protect all wild things. The situation does, however, provide an opportunity for gardeners

....

Hutcheson Memorial Forest:
A No-Management Policy Invites Management by Invasive Species

Hutcheson Memorial Forest is one of only three remaining old-growth forest fragments left in the state of New Jersey. As one of the last uncut white oak–beech forests in the country, it is listed in the National Park Service's Registry of Natural Landmarks. In the 1950s, core samples proved some of the oaks and beeches to be in excess of 350 years old. The woods were saved from timber harvest by a group of well-intentioned citizens and the local carpenters union, who subsequently donated them to Rutgers, The State University, for research and preservation. In their zeal to protect this precious natural heritage for all time, the groups included unusually restrictive deed covenants containing "no-management" language. These good and careful citizens could not predict that the land around their beloved old-growth woods would become so changed by suburbanization that the protective no-management clause would instead become a curse, as invasive species and herds of deer have proliferated and changed the forest, preventing natural forest regeneration. Where oaks once sprouted, Norway maple is taking over. Wildflowers once carpeted the forest floor; now garlic mustard rules. The formerly rich understory, including dogwood, has been displaced by Japanese honeysuckle, multiflora rose, and Japanese barberry. Instead of a surviving example of a vanishing forest community, Hutcheson Memorial Forest has become a laboratory for what happens to an unmanaged old-growth forest fragment surrounded by human development.

....

Figure 2.12. This elegant member of the lily family, merrybells (*Uvularia sessilifolia*), was until recently a common woodland wildflower. A favored deer food, in many areas it is now nearly impossible to find a blooming specimen.

to play an important role. We cannot fence the deer out of nature preserves, but we can, if we are persistent, keep them out of our gardens. In a strange paradox, our gardens can be safer than a protected area for the plants that deer love best and eat first; these plants are rapidly being extirpated in the wild, especially plants in the lily, orchid, and trillium families (figure 2.12).

One of our oldest American garden plants, the Franklin tree (*Franklinia alatamaha*), would be extinct were it not for the interest of gardeners. Of course, it helps that this small ornamental tree has great garden appeal, producing large, white, camellialike flowers in September, no less. A tree with fewer obvious attributes might already be extinct by now. The bottom line, however, is that gardeners made a difference and a species that might have been lost forever is still with us. If we care to, we can make our gardens serve a larger purpose as sanctuaries for our vanishing wild flora.

This chapter barely scratches the surface of the fascinating world of animal and plant interactions. Gardeners can make a meaningful contribution to science by noting their observations and sharing them. It will take many lifetimes to learn all of the myriad interdependencies sustaining northeastern fields and forests. In the meantime, the wisest policy is to use indigenous plants whenever possible for the benefit of all wildlife.

3

"SAFE SEX"

IN

THE GARDEN

One must battle one's own perceptions.
To our human eyes, bigger fruits are
better, exaggerated flowers more
interesting than modest ones. I lose the
battle often.

....

SARA STEIN, *Noah's Garden*

For the purposes of this book, the phrase *safe sex* means limiting the ability of nonindigenous plants to reproduce on their own. It is the key to minimizing their risk to the larger environment. To successfully implement "safe sex" principles, gardeners need to develop an understanding of plant reproductive strategies. This chapter starts with an explanation of plant names and just enough horticultural terminology to enable a fruitful discussion. As these topics can sometimes be confusing, not least because, unfortunately, the terminology is sometimes misused, definitions are given along with explanations in context. Plant choices and their consequences follow, leading to suggestions for practices that either encourage the indigenous plants we want or discourage an increase in the nonindigenous ones that must be controlled.

UNDERSTANDING SCIENTIFIC NAMES

A prerequisite to any in-depth discussion of plants is the basic vocabulary behind plant names (*botanical nomenclature*). Taxonomists, the scientists that name living things, created a system whereby each plant or animal has at least two names. All have a single name (*scientific* or *Latin name*) used by scientists and one or more names used by almost everybody else (*common names*). The use of common names alone is simply inadequate because there are too many common names used for the same plant. Each region seems to have its own variation, and sometimes the same common name is applied to two very different plants (with possible unpleasant consequences if one is edible and the other is not). It is a good idea when purchasing plants (especially if you plan to eat them) to use the scientific name. That is the only way to be sure you actually get the plant you want. The scientific names are supposedly permanent, but hard-working taxonomists occasionally find they need to change a name. At present, asters are undergoing taxonomic revision, and the scientific names have changed, but many nurseries and gardeners (myself included) will cling to the old names as long as possible.

Each scientific name has two parts. The first is the *genus* (plural: *genera*), representing membership in a larger related group of organisms, and the second part, *species* (plural: *species*), refers to the specific organism. Scientific names are full of clues about the plant, including, in some instances, place of origin. It was not uncommon for plant explorers to name plants after the place in which they were found. Take a look at the scientific names of two closely related plants: *Juniperus virginiana* and *Juniperus chinensis*. Both plants belong to the same genus, *Juniperus*, but they are two different species. Without knowing anything more, which species, *virginiana* or *chinensis*, is more likely to be native to North America? *Juniperus virginiana*, commonly known as eastern red cedar, is the correct answer. Though its common name includes the word *cedar*, this hardy evergreen is not, botanically, a true cedar. It does, however, have richly colored, aromatic wood that is used to line cedar chests and closets, and its berries are used to flavor gin. *Juniperus chinensis* is the scientific name for Chinese juniper, obviously native to China as can be inferred from the species name itself.

Similar examples include *Lonicera japonica* (from Japan), and *Asarum europaeum* (from Europe). Less obvious names that frequently indicate European origin are *vulgare*, meaning a common plant, and *officinalis*, a medicinal plant. Familiar examples include many European species that have naturalized here, such as the common oxeye daisy, *Leucanthemum vulgare*, mugwort, *Artemisia vulgaris*, sweet clover, *Melilotus officinalis*, and dandelion, *Taraxicum officinale*. The use of the species name to guess a plant's origin is not infallible, however. (Nothing is ever simple in botany.) *Lathyrus japonicus*, the common beach pea, for example, is indigenous to both the eastern United States and Japan. It is one of the circumboreal plants mentioned in the first chapter that migrated from one continent to another across land bridges in the wake of the glaciers.

A close look at the spellings of the species named above reveals that similar words do not always have the same endings. This is because taxonomy has its basis in, and follows the rules of, Latin; scientific names are also correctly referred to as Latin names. Prior to the emergence of English as an international language, Latin was the language used by educated people in many areas throughout the world to communicate with one another. At present, few users of botanical Latin, myself included, have more than a passing familiarity with Latin and must simply memorize the names as if they were nonsense words, possibly missing out on some useful information in the process.

REPRODUCTIVE PROCESSES IN PLANTS

The second prerequisite to implementing the principles of "safe sex" is an understanding of the processes related to natural plant reproduction and human-engineered plant propagation. Plants are often defined according to the method by which they were produced; we refer to them as hybrids, cultivars, or open-pollinated plants. These are not arbitrary distinctions, as different production methods will result in plants with different genetic characteristics. The following sections provide a brief review of this complex subject.

Pollination

The previous chapter examined pollination from the point of view of the insects that exploited nectar and pollen resources. Here I focus on how the plants benefit from the insects' activities. Although there are different types of pollination, all involve sexual reproduction between male pollen and female plant parts, with the end goal of increased genetic diversity in the offspring. *Cross-pollination* occurs when pollen from one plant pollinates another plant. Not all plants require animal assistants for cross-pollination to occur; many trees and grasses, for example, are wind-pollinated, as pollen is blown haphazardly from male to female flowers. Insect pollinators offer

Figure 3.1. As this wasp sips nectar, it unintentionally pollinates the mountain mint (*Pycnanthemum muticum*), added insurance that the mint's seeds will be fertile.

a slightly more targeted approach, guaranteeing a plant's fertility (figure 3.1). Even plants that are capable of fertilizing themselves (self-fertile) will be more productive if they are cross-pollinated. Anyone who has planted fruit trees is familiar with the fact that the crop will be more bountiful if there are two or more different varieties of fruit available for cross-pollination. Some fruit trees require cross-pollination, because, despite the fact that they have both male and female flowers, they have developed physical barriers to prevent self-fertilization. Wind, insects, and other natural forms of pollination are referred to as *open-pollination*, and result in offspring with the greatest amount of genetic diversity. In contrast, hand-pollination by humans restricts diversity to ensure predictable results for commercial purposes.

Male and Female Plants

Botanists have discovered that plant sexuality is quite complex. Most plants are *hermaphrodites*, plants that have flowers with both male and female parts. A minority of plants have separate male and female flowers that occur on the same individual plant; they are *monoecious*. Plants with separate male and female individuals are the *dioecious* plants; in other words, all of the flowers on a given specimen are either male or female. Common

Figure 3.2. Holly (*Ilex opaca*) is a dioecious plant; in the photo, the female flowers are on the left, and the male flowers are on the right.

examples of dioecious plants are hollies (*Ilex* spp.) (figure 3.2) and the gingko tree (*Gingko biloba*); many more examples are given in appendix D. Such plants cannot be fruitful and multiply without at least two individuals, one of each sex. When purchasing dioecious plants, gardeners can sometimes be confused by instructions to plant many individuals of the same species for good fruit production. This advice has nothing to do with cross-pollination; rather it is because nursery staff often cannot tell male from female at a young age. If the customer buys enough plants, odds are good that both sexes will be represented—not an ideal system from the gardener's point of view, who, for example, may purchase seven plants and later discover that six are male. Purchasing dioecious plants is discussed in more detail in chapter 7.

CULTIVATED PLANT VARIETIES

Within species, genetic diversity creates different forms, variations, even mutations (figure 3.3). If the differences are great enough, botanists will classify the plant as either a *variety* or a *subspecies* of a given species. Many variations are less significant; for example, a flower in the wild may exhibit a different shade of its usual color. When a plant with an unusual, desirable

Figure 3.3. This black-eyed Susan (*Rudbeckia hirta*) found growing wild in a field displays a natural mutation—not one likely to appeal to the horticultural trade, however.

trait is found, a horticulturist may propagate it as a cultivated variety, or *cultivar*. The many differently named fruit trees are common examples of cultivars, though they are routinely referred to as varieties by the agricultural community. Horticulturists working with many different characteristics of a single species can selectively breed for a wide range of traits, including aesthetics, cold hardiness, and pest- and disease-resistance. Common examples of naturally occurring variations are yellow-berried hollies, bicolored or banded mountain laurels, and pendulous or weeping forms of trees.

Plant breeders work with these and other distinctive traits to create all shades and combinations of colors and forms, often bestowing fancy names on their new creations, in much the same spirit as dog and cat breeders. An article in the Brooklyn Botanic Garden's newsletter referred lightheartedly to cultivars as "plant pets." Many cultivars would never have come into being without human intervention. Reproducing them is complex, because in order to retain their unique characteristics, cultivars must usually be asexually propagated or *cloned*. The following examples demonstrate how scientific naming rules distinguish natural varieties from cultivars. The pink dogwood, considered a distinct variety of the common white flowering dogwood by botanists, is called *Cornus florida* var. *rubra*; a cultivar of that variety is called *Cornus florida* 'Cherokee Chief.'

44

Figure 3.4. This hybrid magnolia, 'Hattie Carthan,' is one of several bred for improved cold hardiness, crossing cucumber magnolia (*Magnolia acuminata*), indigenous to the Northeast, with Asian magnolias.

Hybrid Plants

A hybrid plant is the result of interbreeding between two closely related species, usually within the same genus. This can occur naturally in the wild between, for example, two different species of oak trees or two different species of azaleas. Unlike hybrid animals, many hybrid plants can, and do, reproduce. Horticulturists purposefully create and interbreed hybrids in the same ways and for the same reasons that varieties are selected and bred. Hybrids can be created that would never occur in the wild because their parents evolved on separate continents. Asian or European species crossed with American species have resulted in hybrids commonly used in both horticulture and agriculture, for example, many rhododendrons, magnolias, and grapes (figure 3.4). Botanical nomenclature indicates hybrids and their parents with a small × as follows: *Quercus marilandica* × *Q. phellos* (blackjack oak crossed with willow oak) produces the offspring known as *Quercus* × *rudkinii*, or Rudkin's oak. Newly created hybrids are often identified only by the fancy names given by the breeder, because in some cases the parentage may be quite complex or even unknown. For example, the popular hybrid azalea 'Nacoochee,' the product of a cross between two hybrid parents, may be listed in catalogs simply as "Azalea 'Nacoochee.'" In such cases, it will be necessary to consult a text on azaleas or the Internet if you want to know the actual plant parents.

Hybrid Cultivars

Once a hybrid is selected and named, it, too, is considered a cultivar and, like the others, is usually cloned for distribution. A consistent problem with hybrid cultivars is the failure by nurseries and sometimes even the plant breeders themselves to identify the parentage of a given plant, or even to specify that it is a hybrid, rather than a variety of a single species. The problem seems to be rooted in an industrywide state of confusion between these two types of cultivars. For example, I frequently come across mountain laurel (*Kalmia latifolia*) cultivars referred to as hybrids in nursery catalogs, when in fact, as there is only one species of mountain laurel, all are varieties of the same species. Numerous failed attempts to create hybrids between different members of the genus *Kalmia* have been well documented by noted mountain laurel breeder Richard Jaynes.

Owing to their often complex parentage, it is more difficult to predict the effects on the surrounding landscape of cultivars that are hybrids. For example, an indigenous host plant that is crossed with a related but nonindigenous plant may no longer provide edible food for the caterpillars that depend on it. In contrast, cultivars that are simply varieties of a single species are unlikely to vary too much from their open-pollinated relatives. For this reason, I will refer to the hybrids separately as *hybrid cultivars* and limit the use of the term *cultivar* to varieties of a single species.

CHOOSING BETWEEN CULTIVARS
AND OPEN-POLLINATED INDIGENOUS PLANTS

While it is always most desirable from an ecological point of view to plant open-pollinated indigenous species, unfortunately, it is not always practical. Few gardeners have access to indigenous plants propagated from local sources and there are laws prohibiting people from simply digging and removing plants from protected areas. Particularly if there are no regional sources of open-pollinated plants, the primary benefit of preserving local genetic diversity may be nullified by problems caused by introducing genetic material from farther away. Cultivars of indigenous plants are certainly no better in this respect; their main advantage lies in their availability, and many are now offered at retail garden centers. From a pragmatic point of view, if gardeners were given the choice between two indigenous plants, one open-pollinated and the other a cultivar of the same species, many would be just as likely to pick the open-pollinated plant as the cultivar, especially if the open-pollinated plant was less expensive. The problem lies in the fact that cultivars are often the only indigenous plants available at many garden centers. The choice between an indigenous cultivar and a nonindigenous plant is an easy one, from my perspective, because although the impact of cultivars on the larger environment is open to question, the impact of non-indigenous plants is known, and the news is not good.

Cultivars offer many benefits. In the first place, they are readily available at local nurseries, and they cannot possibly have been collected in the wild, because they are nursery creations. Some of the larger indigenous plants are showy, exciting plants, but they may simply be too large for the smaller garden; dwarf cultivars solve that problem. With new introductions coming out every year, they satisfy both the gardener's quest for novelty and the nurseries' need to market new varieties of plants. Almost certainly, they pose less of a threat to natural areas; there have been no reports of any invasive indigenous cultivars. Last and most important, they already fit into the food web; cosmetic changes such as height or flower color should have no bearing on leaf chemistry.

Compared with open-pollinated indigenous plants, though, cultivars do come up short. Some may have been selected from populations in the southern part of their range and may not be as reliably cold hardy as plants from northern populations. The cultivars with a showy, double layer of petals (double-flowered) are usually sterile and have little or no nectar. The information provided by a nursery concerning the origins of a particular cultivar is often inadequate to determine whether or not the plant is a hybrid and, if so, the species of the hybrid's parents. Finally, because nearly all must be vegetatively propagated, they typically lack genetic diversity.

Some of these problems can be ameliorated by avoiding the overuse of any single cultivar. Particularly if the species is short-lived and you are hoping it will self-sow, planting two or more cultivars will make cross-pollination possible and will greatly improve your chances of success. I know of at least one enterprising nursery that sells three different cultivars of smooth withe rod (*Viburnum nudum*), including the most popular, 'Winterthur,' together as a package to ensure that the shrubs bear colorful fruit for their customers. Fortunately, more plant breeders are working with indigenous plants, and for many species there are literally a dozen or more cultivars to choose from. If possible, choose a variety of different ones, rather than several individuals of the same cultivar. Careful choice of a variety of cultivars may allow for an overlapping but extended period of bloom and a more natural, less monochromatic, color scheme.

CHOOSING BETWEEN DIFFERENT TYPES OF HYBRID CULTIVARS

First, it is important to distinguish between those offspring produced by two indigenous parents and those produced from one indigenous and one nonindigenous parent (the latter is by far the more common scenario). Although hybrid cultivars resulting from crosses between two indigenous species may share the same drawbacks as cultivars of one species, there is no reason to suspect that local insects would find them unpalatable. On the other hand, hybrids from crosses between one indigenous and one nonindigenous parent may have an unfamiliar element introduced into their leaf chemistry that might make them unpalatable to insects that use the indigenous parent as a host species. Without testing new hybrids, we simply do not know, because each one may be different. In terms of invasiveness, hybrids, generally speaking, do not produce an abundance of viable seeds. Some hybrids are known to be completely sterile. That can be an advantage if you want a particular plant for its physical attributes and you do not want to worry that the plant will naturalize. When in doubt, however, it is safest to assume that a hybrid plant can and will reproduce. For this and other reasons, it is best not to overuse hybrids. The same positive factor that may guard against an ability to naturalize also means reduced or nonexistent resources for pollinators and other wildlife.

CHOOSING BETWEEN INDIGENOUS AND NONINDIGENOUS PLANTS

Virtually every American garden already contains plenty of nonindigenous species. By an overwhelming margin, the majority of plants offered for sale by nurseries will be nonindigenous. Knowing the consequences of their overuse, carefully weigh every decision to introduce more of them. Use nonindigenous plants in the garden as you might use a particularly pungent spice when cooking, that is, sparingly. Consider the functions and ornamental values of the nonindigenous plants you might want to purchase and look for indigenous species that can perform in similar fashion. Chapter 5 offers some specific guidance in this respect. The ultimate landscape goal should be a stunningly beautiful garden with an abundance of indigenous plants, along with an occasional nonindigenous plant that carries sentimental or historical value to the gardener. This is the polar opposite of what we now have.

When using indigenous species in the garden, increasing the number of plants through reproduction usually is seen as a positive outcome. Seedlings may not always appear exactly where you want them, but they are easy enough to move. In contrast, the goal with nonindigenous plants is to eliminate uncontrolled reproduction, which, as we have seen, can have negative consequences for the surrounding environment. The motto of the responsible gardener, with regard to nonindigenous plants, should be "What grows in my garden, stays in my garden." The following section is offered knowing that gardeners occasionally will find certain nonindigenous plants irresistible. The principles listed below are offered to guide more responsible choices and reduce the chance that the nonindigenous plants selected will cause significant problems.

PRINCIPLES OF "SAFE SEX" IN THE GARDEN

✓ **Most of the trees we plant will outlive us—choose wisely; choose indigenous.**

As we know, it is impossible to "deadhead" a tree; nonindigenous trees may produce seeds for a hundred years or more. Fortunately, the Northeast is blessed with many species of long-lived, majestic shade trees and lovely flowering ornamental trees. There is a chart in Douglas Tallamy's book *Bringing Nature Home* showing that indigenous species of trees in just ten genera (oaks, willows, and cherries are the top three) provide food for well over a thousand species of butterfly and moth caterpillars. Along with other insect larvae, the butterfly and moth caterpillars feeding on indigenous trees are themselves food for more than 96 percent of baby birds. Before choosing a new tree, consider how many life forms, in addition to humans, will be able to use it over the next hundred years (figure 3.5).

Figure 3.5. Plant indigenous trees to lure Silk moths like this splendid Cecropia (*Hyalophora cecropia*), with its five- to six-inch wing span.

✓ **When choosing nonindigenous plants, be wary of recent introductions.**

Avoid the urge to be the first on your block to own Oriental weeping buttonbush. This is not just a question of escaped seedlings that may naturalize; especially with new introductions, there is a very real risk of introducing new pathogens and pests. According to author Robert Preston, writing in the December 10, 2007, *New Yorker*, there are strong indications that the hemlock wooly adelgid (*Adelges tsugae*) was shipped from Asia to Richmond, Virginia, probably around 1911, by a gardener who imported conifers for her Japanese garden. Acres of giant hemlocks throughout the Great Smokies and other Appalachian forests are now standing like skeletons, bare of their evergreen needles, all life sucked out of them by tiny white fluffballs. There seems to be no stopping the hemlock woolly adelgid, which is killing hemlocks farther and farther north, its spread aided by global warming.

In 1911, no one knew any better; now we do know, and we continue to repeat history. At present, the nursery industry is grappling with a dire threat to our oak trees. A soil-borne root disease, sudden oak death (caused by the pathogen *Phytophthora ramorum*), has killed tens of thousands of trees in the Pacific Northwest and California. The disease continues to be spread around the country on infected nursery stock. Try to satisfy the urge for novelty by collecting brand new cultivars of your favorite indigenous plants.

(Some of us may need to join Plant Collectors Anonymous. It is no accident that I have planted more than two hundred different cultivars of indigenous plants in my own garden.)

✓ **Avoid using plants identified as invasive species.**

Some plants are not safe to use under any conditions, for example, Oriental bittersweet (*Celastrus orbiculatus*), porcelain berry (*Ampelopsis brevipedunculata*), purple loosestrife (*Lythrum salicaria*), Norway maple (*Acer platanoides*), Callery pear (*Pyrus calleryana*), Japanese barberry (*Berberis thunbergii*), and all of the nonindigenous honeysuckles (*Lonicera* spp.). There are federal, state, and regional lists of invasive species. It is a good idea to become familiar with the plants on these lists, although there can be a long lag time between updates, so plants recently found to cause problems may not yet be included. With rare exceptions, these lists have no regulatory effect, so, amazingly, nurseries continue to sell the plants as long as unwary consumers continue to purchase them. Chapter 4 discusses known invasive species still found in many, if not most, nurseries, and alternative indigenous plants to use in their place.

✓ **Avoid plants that use certain reproductive strategies.**

Some of the most notorious invasive plants, including many of those listed in the previous paragraph, produce prolific quantities of seeds and berries, and they have dependable sources of transport in the form of wind and birds. Be wary of all nonindigenous plants that produce berries or have seeds that are wind-dispersed. Also avoid *stoloniferous* plants, those that reproduce vegetatively by sending out stolons or runners. Examples include kudzu (*Pueraria montana* var. *lobata*), English ivy (*Hedera helix*), and Chinese and Japanese wisteria (*Wisteria sinensis* and *W. japonicus*). Not only are these plants a danger to the surrounding landscape, but they are a colossal nuisance to the gardener. I have personally tried for fifteen years to rid my garden of the goutweed (*Aegopodium podagraria*) I inherited from previous owners, a groundcover that spreads by deep underground runners. Stoloniferous plants also reproduce by seeds; if you have any of them in your garden, make sure to keep them from producing seeds. English ivy is a particular problem in this respect. Many people let the plant climb trees; the vines harm trees by robbing them of water and nutrients, and weighing down branches (figure 3.6). As the vines climb the tree, they gain access to enough sunlight to flower and produce berries that are readily eaten by birds that

Figure 3.6. English ivy is literally starving the life out of these trees from the ground upward. As it advances, it destroys the lower branches first, leaving only tufts of leaves from the very top of the tree to gather energy from the sun.

spread the seeds far from their original source. Homeowners often have no idea that their English ivy is producing seeds. Vine-covered trees also are far more prone to storm damage.

✓ Use only male dioecious plants.

This principle is solidly established and is undoubtedly one reason that gingkos have not yet naturalized in the New York metropolitan region. Gingkos are tough, attractive trees, well-suited to the urban environment, and many male gingkos have been planted throughout New York City. Because female gingkos bear fruit that, when ripe, gives off a nauseating odor, they have been systematically weeded out by plant nurseries. Perhaps if the large seed clusters of the female tree-of-heaven (*Ailanthus altissima*) had the same odor problem, they would not have been allowed to overrun the region. A large population of both males and females is present, unfortunately, and the tree-of-heaven has successfully naturalized along highway rights-of-way from urban to suburban areas. Only if the females of a dioecious species can successfully be excluded from a population, as in the case of gingkos, will the species be prevented from naturalizing.

✓ **Use annuals.**

Unlike long-lived perennials, true *annuals* complete their entire life cycle in one growing season. Another category, the *tender annuals*, are actually perennials indigenous to much warmer climates; they perish at the first sign of frost. Most annuals are colorful, dependable additions to the landscape and their lack of persistence makes them less of a threat to the surrounding environment. Some will self-sow, and those are best avoided. A word of caution: As global warming progresses, gardeners must be alert for changes in plant habits as our climate zones keep changing. Some of those tender annuals may become capable of overwintering and naturalizing. For the time being, however, many annuals, such as garden impatiens (*Impatiens walleriana*), in common use for many years, show no signs of becoming invasive.

✓ **Use heirloom plants.**

In theory, plants that were introduced two or three centuries ago and have not, in the intervening years, been observed to naturalize, would seem to be relatively safe choices, especially compared with more recent introductions. In practice, however, after a sobering bit of research, I was left with a very short list of nonindigenous plants that have not naturalized somewhere in the eastern United States. In general, I found that species were more likely to have naturalized than hybrids, so, at least in the case of plants, well-bred may equal well-behaved. The short list in table 3.1 is certainly not exhaustive, and I encourage readers to research further any plants of interest.

✓ **Use sterile plants.**

I am still hoping that the nursery industry will produce truly sterile clones of the Norway maple and Callery pear (or simply stop producing them altogether). Unfortunately, the industry has concentrated on producing sterile clones of indigenous trees, in order to avoid "messy" seeds and berries. We are dependent on the nursery industry to produce sterile plants before we can buy them. Even then, we must be wary. Hybrids cannot be presumed to be sterile. Claims were made that certain cultivars of the rogue plant purple loosestrife, for example, 'Morden Pink' and 'Dropmore Purple,' were sterile; field research has proven those claims to be false. Some of the showier cultivars and hybrids of common perennials, particularly so-called double forms (with extra petals and no true flowers in the center), are known to be sterile (figure 3.7). Of course, a garden too full of eye-popping, double-flowered blooms with no nectar will be a terrible disappointment to foraging butterflies. Although sterile forms solve the problem of invasiveness, they take up precious garden space and contribute nothing in the way of nectar or other foods for insects and other wildlife.

Table 3.1.
Time-Tested Heirloom Flowers

The nonindigenous plants listed below have been in use for more than a century, in some cases far longer, and have not been documented to spread outside of cultivation. While they cannot serve as productive members of the regional food web, compared with invasive nonindigenous plants, they may be a relatively harmless addition to the garden.

Shrubs and Vines

Hydrangea anomala subsp. petiolaris, climbing hydrangea
Rosa cvs. (avoid species roses), hybrid rose
Syringa vulgaris, lilac

Annuals, Bulbs, and Perennials

Astilbe chinensis, astilbe
Campanula medium, Canterbury bells
Canna hybrids (cvs. in Italian and Premier groups), canna lilies
Cobaea scandens, cup-and-saucer vine
Epimedium × versicolor, barrenwort
Gladiolus lemoinei, gladiolus
Hemerocallis lilio-asphodelus, lemon lily
Impatiens cvs. and hybrids, annual impatiens
Iris cvs. and hybrids, bearded irises
Lavandula latifolia or *L. stoechas* hybrids (not *angustifolia*), lavenders
Lilium candidum, madonna lily
Molucella laevis, bells of Ireland
Paeonia cvs. and hybrids, peonies
Petunia × hybrid cvs., petunias
Trapaeolum majus, nasturtium
Tulipa cvs. (avoid *Tulipa sylvestris*), tulip
Zaluzianzkya capensis, night-blooming phlox
Zinnia elegans (avoid *Z. violacea*), zinnia

Figure 3.7. This double-flowered bloodroot (*Sanguinaria canadensis*) is lovely but sterile, as the extra petals have replaced the interior nectar-producing flower parts.

✓ **Use only a single specimen, as an accent.**

Planting only a single specimen may make reproduction less successful, particularly if the plant requires cross-pollination. Where large masses of the same plant are required, such as hedges and shrub borders, plants known to be sterile, or males only would be slightly better choices, whereas indigenous species would definitely make the best choice.

✓ **Stick with just one cultivar.**

So, despite all this good advice, you simply cannot resist a large group planting of nonindigenous miscanthus (*Miscanthus sinensis*) grass, or something else equally likely to spread uncontrollably. If you stick to just one clone or cultivar, it may be unable to reproduce, again because there will be no cross-pollination; all of the clones will be genetically identical. This is a risky strategy and you will need to thoroughly explore your neighborhood to make sure that other neighborhood gardens do not already have a different cultivar of the same species. The strategy still may not work if your neighbors decide that imitation is the sincerest form of flattery. Next spring they may accidentally bring home the nursery's brand new miscanthus cultivar. In that case, please see the section on maintenance, below, under "Deadhead."

....

Principles of "Safe Sex" in the Garden

Most of the trees we plant will outlive us—choose wisely; choose indigenous. When selecting nonindigenous plants, apply the following guidelines:

✓ Be wary of recent plant introductions.
✓ Avoid using plants identified as invasive species.
✓ Avoid plants that use certain reproductive strategies.
✓ Use only male dioecious plants.
✓ Use annuals.
✓ Use heirloom plants.
✓ Use sterile plants.
✓ Use only a single specimen, as an accent.
✓ Stick with just one cultivar.

....

MAINTENANCE: PREVENTING REPRODUCTION IN NONINDIGENOUS PLANTS

✓ Deadhead.

Many gardeners are familiar with the technique of removing spent flowers before they produce seeds but consider it an optional task, perhaps only for the overly fussy gardener. When using nonindigenous plants in the garden, protection of the surrounding landscape dictates mandatory deadheading. Entire books have been written about deadheading and other perennial maintenance issues. In many cases, deadheading will actually improve the look of your garden, and you may get another set of blooms to reward you. It is easy to be dedicated to deadheading. Nothing is more pleasant than strolling through your garden on a picture perfect day enjoying the masses of butterflies nectaring on your indigenous plants and clipping spent blossoms from the very few nonindigenous plants you simply could not resist.

✓ Remove invasive trees.

Obviously, no gardener can kill any plant he or she does not own. Assume, however, that you own a Norway maple, for example. As there is no way to deadhead a tree, it is reasonable to consider taking it down. This is weeding on a giant scale, but consider how many seedlings you and your neighbors have to pull and what an unpleasant task that is. Think about all the seedlings you see sprouting along the roads nearby. Taking down large trees can be expensive, but you do not have to cut the tree down to kill it. There is a technique called *girdling*. If you remove a section of bark all the way around a tree, you disrupt its ability to pull water and nutrients up into the crown and the tree will die. That tree becomes beneficial for local wildlife, and girdling is, in fact, a deliberate wildlife management strategy in many forests. The amount of "standing dead wood" is one measure of a given forest's wildlife habitat suitability. Woodpeckers and others will find food and shelter in the dying and ultimately decaying tree. This technique is obviously inappropriate for any tree near the house, but may be perfectly acceptable in the backyards and woodlots of larger residential properties. All maples are notorious root sprouters and will send out live shoots either from the stump, if the tree was cut, or the section below the point at which the tree has been girdled. Unless you have a fence, deer will likely finish off the sprouts in a season or two, provided that the tree was cut low enough for them to browse. In the absence of deer, burning the cut area with a propane torch (more than one application may be needed) usually takes care of the problem. Other invasive trees worthy of control efforts include the dioecious tree-of-heaven. Fortunately, less work is involved, because only the females need to be removed.

✓ Practice weeding and related forms of control.

Closely related to deadheading is the method of weeding, known colloquially as *weed whacking*, advocated by noted landscape architect Larry Weaner. The tool of choice is, of course, a weed whacker (string trimmer). The theory behind Weaner's method is that if the plant cannot use its leaves to photosynthesize, it will eventually die, even if you leave the roots in the ground. I am currently giving the weed whacking method the acid test on my goutweed, which still comes up from beneath the layers of oak leaves and pine needles with which I have tried to smother it. (Unfortunately, after one full growing season of the combined weed whacking/smothering treatment, the goutweed is still sending up new leaves in many places, which proves just how persistent this plant is, and why you do not want it in your garden.) Another valid point Weaner makes about weeding is that if you pull a weed out with its roots, you have opened the soil up to light and weed seeds, inviting new invasions.

There is one class of plants, however, that resist weed whacking, and must be pulled, either by hand or with a mechanical weed-puller, unless you can resign yourself to living with them. These are the basal-leaved plants such as dandelions, hawkweeds (*Hieracium* spp.), carpet bugle (*Ajuga* spp.), and crabgrass (*Digitaria* spp.). You can weed whack the tops of their little heads off and even scruff up the leaves a bit with the weed whacker, but they will sprout right back, flower, and go to seed the minute you turn your back on them. Water first to loosen the soil, then pull.

The easiest way to cut your chores is to limit the number of plants defined as weeds. It is a good idea to get to know them before you decide to devote precious gardening time to controlling them. Do not assume that every plant that shows up unannounced bearing scruffy leaves is, in fact, a weed. Knowledgeable gardeners recognize and welcome the indigenous wild-flowers that *volunteer* to come into the garden on their own. Some of my favorites, such as daisy fleabane (*Erigeron annuus*), white snakeroot (*Eupatorium rugosum*), and blue heart-leaved aster (*Aster cordifolius*), are in my garden because I watched them instead of weeding them. Daisy fleabane will only volunteer; I know of no commercial source for this lovely, cloud-like indigenous annual. White snakeroot is a beautiful and useful plant, possibly the only perennial that deer really do not like. Many people routinely weed out plants they do not know, especially plants in the daisy family that have coarse leaves and save their flowers for the fall. Wait for the flowers; once you have seen them, you may decide to encourage more volunteers.

In my garden, I define weeds as any nonindigenous plant. However, the list of weeds I try to actively control is a much smaller subset. My mental list is prioritized according to invasiveness, so that purple loosestrife, garlic mustard and, now, Japanese stiltgrass (*Microstegium vimineus*), are at the top, with crabgrass and dandelions way down near the bottom. Most years, the invasive plants take up so much time that I never make it to the bottom of the list. The hardest part of weeding, however, for me at least, is taking out the indigenous plants that just happen to grow in the wrong place. That is what comes of impulses to tidy up the garden. Sometimes, they are so beautiful that I just let them grow. And sometimes, that wrong place turns out to be the perfect place.

SHOWY

SUBSTITUTES

FOR

COMMON

INVASIVE PLANTS

When it comes to the diversity of life,
we can have it all, but we cannot have all of it everywhere.

....

YVONNE BASKIN, *"Nature's Space Invaders"*

With their amazing capacities for reproduction, invasive nonindigenous plants are the gifts that keep on giving. Some of the very worst ones that continue to plague us fortunately are not commercially available, for example, garlic mustard (*Alliaria petiolata*), Japanese stiltgrass (*Microstegium vimineus*), and the notorious kudzu vine (*Pueraria montana* var. *lobata*). Although it is important to be able to recognize and control these and other invasives if they come into either your garden or the local park, there are many sources, some listed at the end of this chapter, that supply identification photographs and suggested management techniques. This chapter instead concentrates on ways to avoid purchasing invasive nonindigenous species that, unfortunately, are still sold by nurseries and specified by landscape designers (some of whom should know better). These plants are listed in appendix E and described below. For each nonindigenous invasive species described, suggestions are made for indigenous plants that would make appropriate substitutes, from both an aesthetic and functional point of view. Without turning this book into another of the many fine native plant encyclopedias already available (some are recommended in the bibliography), this chapter provides a starting point for further research.

Table 4.1.

Using Congeners to Find Alternatives

Nonindigenous	Indigenous
Aesculus hippocastanum, horse chestnut	*Aesculus flava*, yellow buckeye OR *Aesculus parviflora*, bottlebrush buckeye
Callicarpa dichotoma, Japanese beautyberry	*Callicarpa americana*, American beautyberry
Hydrangea paniculata, panicled hydrangea	*Hydrangea arborescens*, snowball hydrangea
Rhamnus cathartica, common buckthorn or *Rhamnus frangula*, glossy buckthorn	*Rhamnus caroliniana*, Carolina buckthorn
Sorbus aucuparia, European mountain ash	*Sorbus americana*, American mountain ash
Spiraea japonica, Japanese spiraea	*Spiraea tomentosa*, meadowsweet
Taxus cuspidata, Japanese yew	*Taxus canadensis*, American yew

Plant descriptions are organized according to size, from the tallest trees to the lowest groundcovers, and within those groups, in most cases, according to season of bloom. Because of their relatively long life spans, emphasis is placed on trees and shrubs at the expense of herbaceous plants. In recommending alternatives, I have tried to highlight plants that may be unfamiliar and deserving of greater attention. Where possible, I have also tried to simplify the process of finding appropriate substitutes through the use of related species, for example, recommending red maple (*Acer rubrum*) as a replacement for Norway maple (*Acer platanoides*). These two species share the same genus and are examples of *congeners* (different species in the same genus). Frequently, congeners share similar traits; an indigenous species often makes an appropriate alternative to a nonindigenous congener. Because many nonindigenous plants are not covered by this book, congeners can be a useful tool for finding indigenous substitutes, as table 4.1 illustrates. By the end of this chapter, it should become apparent that there was never any need to import many of the plants we currently use for landscaping. Their close relatives were already here, waiting to be discovered.

TREES

Norway Maple (*Acer platanoides*)

Norway maple is well adapted to its home territory. The tree leafs out early, with large, thick leaves that shade out competition, and it produces an abundance of seeds. Those seeds can sprout in sun or shade. Its roots may even produce toxic chemicals that further limit competition. This is undoubtedly a rare set of survivalist features, useful for a tree that grows in Norway, where days are short and nights are long. When the tree grows in Brooklyn, however, that is a different story. Norway maple was imported to the United States by John Bartram for landscaping purposes and was used extensively in the creation of New York City's Central Park, as well as many other urban parks and gardens throughout the Northeast. The trees did well in our climate, producing bountiful crops of windborne seeds that soon found their way into every road cut and vacant lot.

Before long, it also turned out that no natural area was safe from aggressive Norway maple seedlings. Because Norway maple leafs out much earlier than any indigenous maple, with larger and thicker leaves, its seedlings and saplings gain a head start of weeks in the spring sunshine. When indigenous forest trees finally leaf out, they face unusual competition for light, water, and nutrients on their own home turf. Not only is the health of the forest canopy undermined, but the flowering plants of the forest floor, especially spring ephemerals, are deprived of the light they need to complete their short life cycles (figure 4.1). In autumn, Norway maple is one of the very last trees to lose its leaves, allowing it to gather and store more energy from the sun. Within the past fifty years, scientists have documented incursions by Norway maple into woodlands and forests formerly presumed safe from invasion owing to their undisturbed quality. A team of researchers in Massachusetts led by Robert Bertin concluded that because of its invasive qualities, together with its excessive use for landscaping purposes, Norway maple poses a significant threat to northeastern woodlands. Recently, the state of Massachusetts took action to ban the sale or distribution of this tree.

Norway maple appears much like a sugar maple during the summer; in fact, many people assume that they are sugar maples. Lacking the sugar and the red maple's brilliant fall colors, however, Norway maple's late autumn yellows are a telltale disappointment. If you have any doubt as to whether or not a maple in question is a Norway maple, the surest way to identify it

Figure 4.1. Another of the spring ephemerals, Dutchman's breeches (*Dicentra cucullaria*), completes its life cycle just as the indigenous trees finish leafing out.

is to pull a leaf from the twig and look for milky white sap. Indigenous maples will have clear sap. (If there is no sap, it may already be too late in the season to perform this test.) This comparison is visible evidence of the enormous differences in leaf chemistry between northeastern maples and Norway maple. Few indigenous insects can use this plant. The nursery industry was quick to pick up on the pest-free characteristic, one reason that it was so widely distributed. A forest overrun with Norway maples cannot support either viable insect or bird populations, because it is not part of the surrounding food web.

In the face of masses of scientific data showing that Norway maples are undermining the health of regional forests, the fact that Norway maple is still one of the most popular trees in commerce is a testament to the nursery industry's inability to implement its own voluntary codes of conduct, drafted in 2001 at the Missouri Botanical Garden. Trees live a long time, and Norway maple is possibly the single worst nonindigenous tree you could choose to plant. If you care about natural woodlands, do not plant a Norway maple.

Appropriate Alternatives

Chokecherry (*Prunus virginiana*) 'Canada Red.' It is difficult to see why anyone would prefer the relatively plain Norway maple to the indigenous maples, with their splendid fall foliage. The one exception that comes to mind is the showy, purple-leaved Norway maple cultivar 'Crimson King,' which may currently hold the title as the nation's best-selling tree. Always popular in cemeteries, as the rather somber shade of plum adds an appropriate touch of color, it is now popular in home landscapes. My candidate to replace the purple-leaved Norway maples is a particularly beautiful variety of the common chokecherry that has purple leaves, called 'Schubert's Red' or 'Canada Red' (color plate 1). It will be hard for any tree to beat the combination of toughness and showy characteristics found in 'Canada Red.' It is smaller than a maple, maturing somewhere between thirty and forty feet, a benefit in modern congested landscapes. It is a much more interesting tree than 'Crimson King,' as it flowers in spring with white flower clusters shaped like bottlebrushes dangling from bright green leaves. As spring progresses, the leaves evolve from lighter to darker green, then the leaves are suffused by purple until by June they are much the same shade as either the Norway maple 'Crimson King' or any of the nonindigenous purple-leaf plums (*Prunus cerasifera*). At about the same time, the flowers of 'Canada Red' have produced tiny green berries, bright against the plum-colored leaves, which gradually become invisible as they also turn deep purple. Birds assist this process of invisibility by consuming them, one reason that I have not been able to confirm personally reports that the color of these trees comes true from seed.

Maples (*Acer* spp.). When discussing alternatives for the common green Norway maple, any of the indigenous congeners, such as red maple (*Acer rubrum*), sugar maple (*A. saccharum*), silver maple (*A. saccharinum*), or the hybrid between red and silver maples, Freeman's maple (*Acer × freemanii*), would make an excellent substitute. (Avoid the nonindigenous sycamore-leaved maple [*Acer pseudoplatanus*], sometimes offered by nurseries.) All maples, however, including Norway maple, share the shallow-rooted characteristic that causes sidewalks to heave, making them unsuitable as street trees. All indigenous maples are excellent shade trees in the garden landscape, particularly ornamental in the fall. For sheer autumn foliage splendor, it is hard to beat either sugar or red maples. Sugar maple is, of course, the signature tree of New England fall foliage tours. Red maples (color plate 2) have the added advantage of bright red flowers on leafless branches in spring; some individuals also have showy red seeds, giving the tree a second springtime flush of bright red "blooms." Interestingly, silver maple was the most popular maple in early American gardens, favored for its lacy foliage, graceful, almost weeping form, and fast growth. The Freeman's maple hybrids share many of these traits, including more autumn colors than the usual golden color of silver maple leaves. There are even a few lacy-leaved sugar maple cultivars on the market, possibly involving promiscuous silver maples. The lacy-leaved sugar maple that I have ('Sweet Shadow'), does not color up as well as most other sugar maples, leading me to suspect some silver maple in its parentage.

Oaks (*Quercus* spp.). From the point of view of insect diversity, the most beneficial substitute for Norway maple would be any of our numerous indigenous oaks. (Avoid the English oak [*Quercus robur*], frequently offered by nurseries.) As many as 534 species of moths and butterflies use oaks as host plants versus a mere 285 species for the maples. With at least twenty-nine eastern oaks to choose from, it is possible to find an oak for every conceivable landscape situation. There are even natural dwarf oaks, bear oak (*Quercus illicifolia*) and chinquapin oak (*Quercus prinoides*), useful for smaller properties. Pin oaks (*Quercus palustris*), scarlet oaks (*Quercus coccinea*), and some red oaks (*Quercus rubra*) color up beautifully in fall and have the advantage of holding on to their leaves longer than maples. White oaks (*Quercus alba*) have rich wine-colored autumn foliage (color plate 3). Where overhead utility lines are not an obstacle, oaks make excellent street trees because most species are drought resistant and salt tolerant.

American elm (*Ulmus americana*). America's former favorite street tree is happily making a comeback thanks to new disease-resistant cultivars such as 'Princeton' and 'Valley Forge.' These superior trees were bred and/or found by devoted horticulturists who refused to give up on the elm after most were killed off by Dutch elm disease (caused by the fungus *Ophiostoma ulmi*). Elms are used as hosts by twenty-one species of moths and butterflies. Nothing beats elm for giving roads that cathedral ceiling look, although today's utility lines unfortunately may occasionally preclude their use. Elms also make terrific backyard trees. As substitutes for Norway maple, they are particularly apt; Norway maples were often used to replace dying elms.

Tulip tree (*Liriodendron tulipifera*). This stately shade tree is a member of the magnolia family, with lovely tulip-shaped flowers of yellow and orange that attract all manner of insects. It is also the host plant for one of our loveliest Silk moths, the Tulip-Tree moth (*Callosamia angulifera*). Exhibiting possibly the most consistently straight, almost columnar, trunk of any deciduous tree, it is also naturally high-branching, making it well suited for formal allées (tree-lined alleys). An excellent example of a tulip tree allée can be found at the New York Botanical Garden; the catface-shaped leaf is the garden's emblem. The species is one of the tallest eastern trees, but creative horticulturists are breeding more compact tulip trees for home gardens, such as 'Ardis' and 'Little Volunteer,' available at better specialty nurseries. While not as brilliant in fall as maple foliage, the tulip tree's leaves turn a lovely shade of pale gold.

Sweetgum (*Liquidambar styraciflua*) and tupelo (*Nyssa sylvatica*). Additional Norway maple substitutes include two other trees that provide excellent shade and give the maples a run for their money come fall foliage time: sweetgum and tupelo (black gum). Sweetgum has lovely star-shaped leaves that turn brilliant scarlet in fall. It does, however, produce hard, spiny seedballs that prevent walking barefoot under the tree. That may be a small price to pay for red, star-shaped foliage. There is a sterile cultivar of sweetgum called 'Rotundiloba,' but as you can probably guess from the name, it has rounded lobes instead of pointed lobes and the star-shaped effect is lost. Tupelo is perhaps the most brilliant of all the scarlet-hued fall foliage (color plate 4). In summer, it has deep green, glossy leaves, quite handsome even before they change color. Only the females produce the tiny berries, so beloved by birds that you may never see them. If you want to be certain your tupelo will have berries, you may want to plant a whole grove of them. Your woods would appear to be aflame in fall.

Callery or Bradford Pear (*Pyrus calleryana*)

No one will believe this, but one of the reasons Callery pear has become the most overused ornamental landscape tree in America is because it has a very predictable form and is easy for landscape architects to draw with an oval template. I learned this as a landscape architecture student; we called them lollipop trees. Like many other fruit-bearing nonindigenous plants, it is invading fields and woodlots throughout its range, outcompeting and displacing indigenous trees, and disrupting the food web because it does not support any insects. It has naturalized in twenty states. The overuse of Callery pear threatens to homogenize the American landscape (not to mention dulling the creative impulses of generations of landscape architecture students).

Bradford pear, the original ornamental pear variety introduced from Asia in the early 1900s, was originally thought to be sterile, but as more new cultivars were released, they began to cross-pollinate Bradford, producing fertile seeds. In some cases, rootstocks on which the cultivars have been grafted will sucker, producing live branches that flower and cross-pollinate flowers on the main stem of the tree. Escaping into disturbed and natural areas, Callery pears grow into dense thickets and can prevent the establishment of natural woodland vegetation. Naturalized offspring of the different cultivars may display varied characteristics, such as branches armed with sharp thorns capable of forming impenetrable barriers.

With their white blossoms in early spring, they do put on quite a show because they bloom before their leaves are open. It is quite a brief show, however; the flowers seldom last long, and the foliage is not particularly interesting. They make poor shade trees, as the same upswept branching pattern that keeps them out of the way of pedestrians and cars offers little relief from the sun. The tight crotch angles are weak spots that eventually succumb to wind and weather. Many horticulturists still consider them ideal, however, for congested urban situations.

Appropriate Alternatives

Chokecherry (*Prunus virginiana*). There is no lack, fortunately, of indigenous ornamental trees that share most, if not all, of the pear's attributes. My candidate for best all-around ornamental pear replacement is the purple-leaved chokecherry 'Schubert's Red' or 'Canada Red' (see color plate 1) mentioned above as a substitute for purple-leaved Norway maples. For those who shudder at the thought of replacing millions of ornamental pears with a tree that turns purple, the common chokecherry that does not turn purple has all of the same attributes listed above and remains a great choice. This tough little tree, for the most part completely ignored by plant breeders, will provide lovely white flowers in spring and tiny red or purple berries in late summer that hang until the birds get them. The leaves display a wide range of fall foliage colors. It is salt tolerant, drought tolerant, and almost seems to look its best in the poorest soils. Chokecherry can be grown in a clump form, tree form, or as a shrub.

When choosing a substitute, if flowering before leaf-out is an important consideration, appropriate trees include redbud (*Cercis canadensis*), dogwoods (*Cornus* spp.), and shadbush (*Amelanchier* spp.), all are described below.

Redbud (*Cercis canadensis*). Commonly available at every garden center, redbud deserves the attention it is finally getting. Under natural conditions, it is found in the understory of moist woodlands; however, it seems to have no problems adjusting to sunny front yards. In spring, leafless branches display multitudes of tiny magenta blossoms, lending a pink glow to the landscape. For those who find the rosy purple blossoms too intense, breeders have been hard at work producing white and soft pink blooming forms of redbud that can now be found in many nurseries. After the blooms fade, redbud trees produce lovely, large, heart-shaped leaves. Breeders have also tinkered with leaf size and color, producing both smaller and gold-colored leaves, among other variations. There are even weeping forms; 'Covey,' for example, is readily available. Perhaps the most stunning redbud cultivar is the purple-leaved clone called 'Forest Pansy.'

Dogwoods (*Cornus florida* and *C. alternifolia*). The large, white blooms of flowering dogwood (*Cornus florida*) are unrivalled in terms of showy spring beauty. Less well-known are the fall displays of bright red berries and brilliant foliage ranging from scarlet to wine (color plate 5). Wild populations in their moist, shady natural habitat have been hard-hit by the recently established anthracnose disease, caused by a fungus; ironically, the fungus is better controlled and the trees are less affected when dogwoods are grown in full sun. In any case, many new disease-resistant cultivars are available, including 'Appalachian Spring.' The traditional branching form of dogwood is open and spreading; newer cultivars seem to be more upright in branching habit; it is difficult to say whether that is the result of pruning, breeding, or growing conditions. Another member of the dogwood family, pagoda dogwood (*Cornus alternifolia*), takes its common name from its attractive horizontal branching pattern. Like flowering dogwood, is has white flowers in spring (blooming after leaves have opened), colorful fall foliage, and berries for the birds. It is more compact than flowering dogwood, making it ideal for smaller landscapes.

Shadbush (*Amelanchier* spp., including *A. arborea*, *A. laevis*, *A. × grandiflora*, and *A. × lamarkii*). Ethereal probably comes closest to describing a shadbush in bloom. The white petals are long and elegant, moving with the slightest breeze. There is even a cultivar, 'Robin Hill,' with pink buds opening to shell-pink blossoms. Most species or natural hybrids bloom before the leaves open or when they are partially open. Some of the most beautiful have copper-colored leaves that remain folded until the blossoms fade; the copper leaves set off the white blossoms to great effect (color plate 6). Under natural conditions, shadbush grows in the forest understory; however, most varieties do well in sunny gardens with adequate moisture.

Kousa Dogwood (*Cornus kousa*)

The practice of recommending Asian Kousa dogwoods and their hybrids instead of flowering dogwood simply because they are resistant to the dogwood anthracnose disease makes sense from only the most narrow horticultural viewpoint. The cause of the anthracnose was identified in the 1990s as a new fungus (*Discula destructiva*). The pattern of its spread, simultaneously attacking both eastern and western indigenous dogwoods near ports of entry separated by an entire continent, together with additional genetic research, strongly suggested that the pathogen was a recent introduction. One possible source is the Asian Kousa dogwood, first introduced in the early 1900s. The species is known to harbor the fungus with few visible effects. While in many parts of the Northeast flowering dogwoods are recovering and proving to be more resistant to the anthracnose than expected, it seems unwise to continue to plant trees that serve as healthy hosts for a pathogen that attacks one of our best-loved and most beautiful forest trees.

Indigenous dogwoods provide nutritious berries for migrating songbirds, but Kousa dogwood berries are much larger, too large for most birds to swallow. The few birds that do tolerate them have already helped the tree to naturalize within New York State. If it is a design requirement to provide a tree that blooms in late spring or early summer, there are many beautiful indigenous trees that flower during this period and that will also provide benefits for many other forms of life.

Appropriate Alternatives

Hawthorns (*Crateagus* spp.). Like Kousa dogwood, hawthorn trees bloom in late spring after their leaves have opened. Hawthorns have lovely white flowers in spring and are particularly useful in the winter landscape, with attractive bark and bright red berries that remain until the birds eat them (color plate 5). Commercially available species and varieties, some thornless, include 'Winter King' green hawthorn (*Crateagus viridis*), cockspur (*C. crus galli*), and Washington hawthorn (*C. phaenopyrum*).

Sweetbay magnolia (*Magnolia virginiana*). Heavenly lemon-scented sweetbay blooms from late June into July. With long, large, glossy leaves and long-petaled ivory flowers, it lends an almost tropical feel to the garden. Frequently sold as bushy, multitrunked clump forms, larger single-trunked specimens are also available; in either form, sweetbay seldom reaches higher than twenty to thirty feet at maturity. Further south, the tree remains evergreen, while here, in mild winters, some leaves may linger.

Purple-Osier Willow (*Salix purpurea*) and Weeping Willows (*S.* × *pendulina and S. sepulcralis*)

Willows are dioecious, one reason they may not invade as rapidly as some others. Many species of European and Asian willows, however, have naturalized throughout the United States. Purple-osier willow, originally planted along streams for erosion control, has naturalized in more than twenty northeastern states. It is still being recommended for that purpose, unfortunately, despite the fact that purple-osier and many other nonindigenous willows have been found to spread along streams, ponds and other wetland areas, crowding out indigenous species. While it may physically hold soil in place along streams, it fails to maintain the terrestrial and aquatic food webs that depend on streamside vegetation. Indigenous willows are host plants for Viceroy (*Limenitis archippus*), Mourning Cloak (*Nymphalis antiopa*), and 454 other butterfly and moth caterpillars.

The traditional use of Far Eastern weeping willows in the landscape may be traced to the widespread use of an antique English china pattern. Many of us, myself included, grew up eating from Blue Willow plates, and the pattern left quite an imprint. When we see a pond, we expect to see a weeping willow next to it. In many golf courses and public parks, the stereotypic pattern of pond and weeping willow is commonplace. Weeping willows are, in fact, culturally restricted to moist sites. Although not considered superaggressive invaders, weeping willows, unfortunately, have naturalized in more than thirty states and can be found invading moist meadows and swales along roadsides.

Appropriate Alternatives

Black willow (*Salix nigra*) and peachleaf willow (*Salix amygdaloides*). These two indigenous willows are reasonable facsimiles of the Asian weeping willows. Both are tall, with similar long, slender willowy leaves. While the branches do not hang quite as pendulously as the weeping willow, the overall effect is similar and is simple to reinforce by training branches downward. Including these two, there are thirty species of indigenous willows to choose from for streamside erosion control. Unfortunately, only a few are commercially available from specialty nurseries, such as prairie willow (*Salix humilis*) and shining willow (*S. lucida*). Indigenous pussy willow (*S. discolor*) can often be found at better garden centers and is recommended as an alternative below.

SHRUBS

Border Forsythia (*Forsythia* spp., *Forsythia* × *intermedia*)

Forsythia is one of the best examples of our homogenized landscape. The widely distributed Asian shrubs are everywhere, nationwide. Forsythia does not show up on most invasive plant lists, although it has naturalized in Indiana, Ohio, and Virginia. Its fruits are capsules rather than berries. The bushes spread slowly by a tenacious root system, becoming gigantic and ungainly without regular pruning. Its long stems root at the tip to form large colonies. Plants covered by forsythia's arching branches are quickly shaded out. A close inspection beneath forsythia usually reveals large patches of bare soil and little else. Its vast root system makes control or removal difficult. Any remaining roots will quickly resprout. One could say, however, that it is well-mannered compared with more rapidly spreading invasive plants. At present, however, forsythia is taking up a disproportionately large amount of real estate without contributing much of anything to other life forms.

Figure 4.2. In addition to providing berries for birds, the spicebush is one of the host plants for the beautiful Spicebush Swallowtail butterfly (*Papilio troilus*), seen here in the photo in its caterpillar stage.

Appropriate Alternatives

Spicebush (*Lindera benzoin*). Forsythia's sole asset is early, bright, spring color. Once it finishes blooming, it is a leggy, nondescript shrub. Fortunately, in our region, spicebush and forsythia bloom at the same time. Spicebush plants have delicate, lightly fragrant yellow blossoms that produce an ethereal effect, as compared with the intense yellow of the forsythias. The tiny yellow flowers appear along the edge of twigs, before the leaves expand, very cheerful after the browns and grays of winter. The deciduous leaves are aromatic, as the plant's name implies. It is a pleasure to brush against them and release their refreshing scent. They glow bright yellow in fall (color plate 7). The female plants produce bright red berries beloved by birds. They are produced from late summer into fall and are high in fats, making them a critical component of the diet of migrant songbirds, as well as residents. Although sources say this shrub can grow as tall as fifteen feet, my mature shrubs have topped out at less than ten feet. Spicebush prefers partial sun or shade and moist to average soil (figure 4.2).

Pussy willow (*Salix discolor*). As a substitute for forsythia, pussy willow provides an earlier spring wake-up call, as it is usually the first to bloom of all northeastern shrubs. (Avoid purchasing the European pussy willows [*Salix caprea* or *S. cinerea*], frequently offered at nurseries.) When I was young, it was our family custom to go out every spring as soon as the snow melted and gather the pussy willow branches with their fresh catkins. (For those who have not experienced this, pussy willow catkins are small, furry, silver buds.) Some branches were left out to dry to be used as everlastings, and some were "forced" in a vase of water until the catkins bloomed with tiny little yellow ribbons. If you are planting a garden with children in mind, pussy willow is an excellent choice. Ruffed Grouse (*Bonasa umbellus*) eat pussy willow buds, and the dense branching habit makes this eight- to fifteen-foot-tall shrub a preferred nesting spot for Goldfinches (*Carduelis tristis*). Seed capsules appear from early to late spring. Pussy willows are tough and adaptable and can be grown in wet or average soils in sun or partial shade.

Japanese Barberry (*Berberis thunbergii*)

A close inspection of barberries in spring will reveal the insignificant flowers, which produce small red berries in fall that are readily consumed by birds and small mammals. Lacking attractive flowers, their function in the landscape is largely utilitarian. Barberries are commonly planted as privacy screens and as hedges and foundation plantings for "traffic" control; people and some animals avoid the thorns. In an attempt to create a more attractive plant, breeders have released several cultivars with purple leaves; these now dominate the market.

Japanese barberry was introduced by botanical gardens beginning in 1896 as a substitute for common barberry (*Berberis vulgaris*), which had been found to harbor an agricultural pathogen, black stem grain rust. It has naturalized in twenty states. Barberries spread to form dense, impenetrable stands, crowding out other plant life. Scientists have documented changes in soil caused by the bushes themselves that help limit competition from indigenous flora. Barberries' thorns protect them from deer; where large herds exist, barberries can take over completely. As the deer continue to eat everything else, at some point, the barberries will be all that is left. The deer will be forced to move on, having literally eaten themselves out of house and home, leaving behind a radically changed landscape. A fine example is clearly visible on the east side of the New York State Thruway in Rockland

County between exits 15 and 16: a decrepit pine plantation overstory with nothing but barberries underneath, as far as the eye can see.

In Connecticut, barberries have recently been identified as a potential public health hazard, as large concentrations of deer ticks infested with Lyme disease have been found on mice living under them. While it is not surprising that the mice that carry ticks would find safe harbor under barberry bushes, it appears that ticks in this environment carry far higher rates of infection. Scientists led by Scott Williams at the Connecticut Agricultural Experiment Station documented rates of infection in ticks found under barberries to be 44 percent compared with ticks on mice found in more natural habitats (only 10 percent). The reasons behind this finding require further exploration, but in the meantime state scientists are actually recommending that barberries be removed. The commonwealth of Massachusetts has already prohibited the sale of Japanese barberries.

Appropriate Alternatives

Brambles (*Rubus* spp.) and other thorn-bearers. Indigenous brambles or raspberries (*Rubus* spp.) and roses (*Rosa virginiana, R. caroliniana*, and *R. setigera*) are good substitutes for creating a dense, thorny hedge. The brambles provide delicious side benefits: blackberries and raspberries; rose hips are also edible. Indigenous roses have lovely pink, sometimes white, fragrant blossoms. For those seriously interested in keeping dogs and people out, nothing beats a carefully pruned shrub hawthorn, such as downy hawthorn (*Crateagus mollis*). For centuries, the British have cultivated enormous, impenetrable hawthorn hedges. Unfortunately, the smaller species of hawthorns are not yet commercially available, although they can be found in some of the better specialty nurseries.

Common ninebark (*Physocarpus opulifolius*). A good alternative for the purple-leaved barberries is common ninebark 'Diabolo,' or the more compact cultivar 'Summer Wine.' Both have lovely white flowers in spring that provide striking contrast with the deep wine-colored, maple-shaped leaves. Plant breeders have been busy with common ninebark, and there are now many interesting colors of foliage to choose from in addition to purple, including lime, gold, and copper (color plate 8). Even when the flowers have faded, the attractive seed clusters appear to "bloom" from afar. After the leaves have fallen, the branches reveal their handsome exfoliating bark. Similar in habit to forsythia and butterfly bush, common ninebark can be pruned to conform to the typical rounded barberry shape, if necessary.

Inkberry (*Ilex glabra*). Another great alternative with evergreen leaves and a naturally rounded shape is inkberry. It is the best replacement for wintergreen barberry (*Berberis julianae*). Inkberry, like all hollies, is dioecious, so if you want the small black berries, make sure to plant both male and female cultivars. Like barberries, inkberry flowers are (visually) nothing to get excited about, but unlike barberries, they are fragrant. At first, it may be difficult to find the source of the heavenly fragrance; once found it is difficult to believe that it can come from such tiny flowers.

Winterberry (*Ilex verticillata*). Barberries have red berries in fall; a far better, showier substitute for this characteristic is winterberry, another member of the holly family. Like all hollies, at least one male plant is needed for the females to produce the showy red berries. Many different cultivars are available to choose from, with different sizes, colors, and densities of berries all along the arching stems. Winterberry is deciduous, and after the leaves fall, the bare branches with their long-lasting, bright red berries are stunning, especially against white snow.

Guelder Rose (*Viburnum opulus*), Siebold Viburnum (*V. sieboldii*), Linden Viburnum (*V. dilatatum*), Doublefile Viburnum (*V. plicatum*), and Wayfaring Tree (*V. lantana*)

Seven species of Eurasian viburnums have naturalized throughout the United States, including the five listed above. Guelder rose, the most widespread, has already spread to thirty states. Virtually all of them have white flowers that produce berries eaten by birds and have been found naturalizing in woods and meadows throughout the Northeast, forming thickets that displace natural vegetation. The adaptable guelder rose threatens to crowd out indigenous viburnums and other plants in a wide variety of habitats, including wetlands. It may hybridize with the American cranberrybush, swamping the natural genetic diversity of the indigenous shrub.

There is an overabundance of hybrids and cultivars of these nonindigenous viburnums available. Nurseries announce the introduction of more new ones every spring, all of which are just as likely as their parent stock to invade the landscape.

Appropriate Alternatives

American cranberrybush (*Viburnum opulus* var. *americanum*). For almost every nonindigenous viburnum, there is an indigenous alternative (table 4.2). The European guelder rose is virtually indistinguishable from its indigenous congener, American cranberrybush (*Viburnum trilobum*). In fact, it is advisable to purchase cranberrybush only from reliable sources, as even some nursery staff have difficulty telling the American and the European species apart from one another. Cranberrybush is, however, worth identifying, as it is quite a beautiful and useful shrub. In bloom, its wide, white flower clusters catch the light with a ring of larger sterile blossoms surrounding the smaller fertile flowers. It has attractive maple-shaped leaves. The large, red berries resemble cranberries and usually remain on the shrubs until late winter, useful for resident birds as well as early-returning migrants. The many other indigenous viburnums are also beautiful and useful shrubs and, like the oaks, there really is one for every landscaping need (figure 4.3).

Table 4.2.
Alternative Viburnums

Nonindigenous	Indigenous
Viburnum dilatatum, linden viburnum	*Viburnum dentatum*, arrowwood
Viburnum lantana, wayfaring tree	*Viburnum lantanoides*, hobblebush
Viburnum opulus var. *opulus*, European cranberrybush or guelder rose	*Viburnum opulus* var. *americanum*, American cranberrybush
Viburnum plicatum, Japanese snowball viburnum	*Viburnum prunifolium*, plum-leaved viburnum
Viburnum rhytidophyllum, leatherleaf viburnum	*Viburnum nudum* var. *cassinoides*, wild raisin
Viburnum setigera, tea viburnum	*Viburnum lentago*, nannyberry
Viburnum sieboldii, Siebold's viburnum	*Viburnum nudum*, smooth viburnum

Figure 4.3. An indigenous viburnum, hobblebush (*Viburnum lantanoides*) is found naturally in the woodland understory and flowers even in full shade.

Nonindigenous Shrub Honeysuckles (*Lonicera spp.*)

The various Eurasian shrub honeysuckles have been around long enough for scientists to have studied well their invasive qualities and their impact on their surroundings. They are extremely easy to propagate, as the landscape industry knows. Any bird can do it, and they do, all over the landscape. Tatarian honeysuckle (*Lonicera tatarica*) was introduced in 1752, the others during the late 1800s. As previously mentioned, they can form dense thickets, crowding out all other plants, and they provide only marginal wildlife habitat. Like other invaders, they green up early in spring and keep their leaves until the very end of autumn. Three of the five honeysuckles listed here already are subject to a sales ban in Connecticut, Massachusetts, and New Hampshire (*L. morrowii*, *L. tatarica*, and *L. × bella*). Connecticut has also banned dwarf honeysuckle (*L. xylosteum*), and, along with Massachusetts, Amur honeysuckle (*L. mackii*). There is a cultivar, 'Red Rem,' which may or may not be subject to the sales ban; if not, it should be, as it has proven to be equally aggressive. The nursery industry, instead of voluntarily discontinuing these highly invasive shrubs, is actively breeding new cultivars. I am betting that the new ones will have either purple or variegated foliage. All of these produce berries readily eaten and spread far and wide by birds; the berries are high in sugars and low in fats and protein. Even the berries of the hybrid Bell's honeysuckle (*Lonicera* × *bella*) contain fertile seeds. Faced with an abundant food source, opportunistic birds will readily make poor food choices; not so very different from humans, really. It is better to remove the temptation and plant better food for birds in our gardens.

Appropriate Alternatives

Deciduous azaleas (*Rhododendron* spp.) Table 2.3 in chapter 2 lists plants that provide higher quality berries, any of which would make excellent substitutes for the invasive honeysuckles. There are indigenous honeysuckle shrubs, for example, American fly honeysuckle (*Lonicera canadensis*) and swamp fly honeysuckle (*L. oblongifolia*) that would also make fine replacements. Unfortunately, they are not commercially available. If the tubular form and fragrance of honeysuckle flowers are the most desirable traits, the deciduous azaleas are unbeatable alternatives. The indigenous swamp azalea (*Rhododendron viscosum*) takes its common name, swamp honeysuckle, from its resemblance to the true honeysuckles, both in flower form and fragrance. Similar but far superior to those of the nonindigenous honeysuckles, the open-throated tubular flowers of our azaleas range in color from white through shades of pink, purple, red, orange and yellow (color plate 9), and many have exceptional fragrance. Flame azalea (*Rhododendron calendulaceum*), has the largest blossoms of them all. Blooming in May, colors range from yellow through orange all the way to copper. As all of our indigenous azaleas hybridize readily in the wild, plant breeders have been inspired to bring us azaleas in a wide range of colors and habits, such that one can have azaleas of many different colors (or even the same color) blooming essentially all season long, from April through September. While a few species, such as swamp honeysuckle, perform better in moist situations, once established, all of the azaleas are quite drought tolerant.

Butterfly Bush (*Buddleia davidii*)

Anyone who has traveled in Great Britain and seen butterfly bush in every weedy corner will not be surprised to learn that it is naturalizing here. Brought from China, each of its showy flower clusters is capable of producing as many as forty thousand tiny, wind-borne seeds. Cultivars of butterfly bush also produce huge amounts of seeds; worse still, their fertility rates reach as high as 92 percent. Seeds remain viable for up to five years. It has already naturalized in seventeen eastern states and is a particular problem on the West Coast, where Oregon is phasing in a complete ban on sales and asking homeowners to deadhead their bushes. Butterfly bush forms dense stands, especially along river banks, crowding out natural vegetation.

While it certainly does attract butterflies with its nectar, researchers have so far not found a single indigenous insect that uses it as a host. Fortunately, we have many indigenous summer-blooming shrubs that also attract butterflies with showy flower plumes to replace the invasive butterfly bush, as well as the invasive chaste tree (*Vitex agnus-castus*) and rose-of-Sharon (*Hibiscus syriacus*).

Appropriate Alternatives

Golden St. John's wort shrubs (*Hypericum* spp.). The best and most enduring of the summer bloomers is a suite of four closely related shrub hypericums, also known as golden St. John's wort. Their common names, unfortunately, do not do them justice: Kalm's St. John's wort (*Hypericum kalmianum*), cedarglade St. John's wort (*H. frondosum*), shrubby St. John's wort (*H. prolificum*), and dense St. John's wort (*H. densiflorum*). Surely one of eastern North America's most beautiful groups of shrubs, they are mystifyingly underappreciated by commercial horticultural interests. Bright golden yellow flowers bloom from early to late summer. And these are no ordinary flowers. The stamens are arranged as eye-catching fluffy yellow balls sitting on top of golden petals. They exhibit a neat, rounded form with simple, blue-green deciduous leaves, attractive seed heads in autumn, and exfoliating reddish-brown bark, adding up to a great garden plant with four-season interest (color plate 10).

Butterflies and other pollinators find these shrubs irresistible. All four species are quite similar in appearance, with cedarglade hypericum having slightly larger flowers. Their blooming periods, however, are staggered. It is quite effective to mass the different species together; to most observers it will appear as one species, but bloom time will extend from early summer right through to the first days of autumn. These spectacular shrubs, useful either as specimens or as shrub borders, usually grow to three feet, although dense St. John's wort may grow to five feet, making them a nice size for com-

Plate 1. Chokecherry 'Schubert's Red.' *Right*, excellent tree form showing full color in late spring; *lower left*, green berries contrast with purple foliage; *upper left*, berries and foliage both purple.

Plate 2. Red maple. *From upper right*, seeds; *lower right*, flowers; and *left*, the tree in spring covered with bright red seeds, giving it the appearance of a second period of "bloom."

Plate 3. Oaks. From *upper right,* white oak in bloom; *lower right,* white oak fall foliage; *left,* scarlet oak in fall.

Plate 4. Tupelo. *Upper right,* in flower; *lower right,* fall foliage; *left,* an older specimen showing the distinctive trunk.

Plate 5. Flowering dogwood and hawthorn. *From upper right,* dogwood berries; *lower right,* dogwood fall foliage; lower left, hawthorn berries; *upper left,* hawthorn blooms.

Plate 6. Shadbush. *From upper right,* blossoms and folded bright copper leaves; *lower right,* flowering before leaves; *lower left,* the pink cultivar 'Robin Hill'; *upper left,* silvery streaks on the bark.

Plate 7. Spicebush. *From upper right,* early spring blossoms; *lower right,* fall foliage; left, shrub in full bloom; *center,* spicebush berries.

Plate 8. Common ninebark species and cultivars. *Upper right,* 'Diabolo'; *lower right,* decorative seed pods; *lower left,* 'Dart's Gold'; *upper left,* 'Coppertina.'

Plate 9. Azaleas. *Upper right*, the hybrid cultivar 'Keowee Sunset'; *lower right*, 'Late Date.' *Left*, Rhododendron calendulaceum 'Smoky Mountaineer' with Tiger Swallowtail butterfly.

Plate 10. Golden St. John's wort. *Upper right*, Tiger Swallowtail on blossom; *lower right*, close-up showing blossom detail; *left*, full-grown shrub blooming in partial shade.

Plate 11. Golden groundsel. *Left,* blooming in masses as a groundcover; *right,* as accents at the edge of a pond, combined with Jacob's ladder.

Plate 12. Geraniums and Jacob's ladder. Groundcovers do not have to be a monoculture. These two low, sprawling, spring-blooming perennials grow into one another with complementary forms and colors.

Plate 13. Asters and goldenrod. A late-fall grouping of the white calico aster, New England aster, and wreath goldenrod (*Solidago caesia*).

Plate 14. Lilies. *Right*, mature Canada lily towering more than six feet high; *lower left*, flower detail; *upper left*, Turk's-cap lily.

Plate 15. Louisiana hybrid irises. *From upper right,* 'Bold Pretender'; *lower right,* 'Creole Flame'; *lower left,* 'Ann Chowning'; *upper left,* copper iris; top center, white blue flag iris.

Plate 16. Grasses. *Upper right,* little bluestem 'The Blues'; *lower right,* purple love-grass; *lower left,* mixed clump of panic grass and Indian grass; *upper left,* a little bluestem meadow; *center top,* the inflorescence, or "flower," of Indian grass.

pact gardens. They will take full sun or part shade. Once established, they are incredibly drought tolerant.

Bottlebrush buckeye (*Aesculus parviflora*). A midsummer bloomer, bottle-brush buckeye sports spectacular upright white panicles that can be more than a foot tall in late summer. Bottlebrush buckeye has distinctive palm-shaped leaves, and its general shape is wider than tall. Over time, it spreads slowly outward from its center, ultimately forming large, showy clumps.

Sweet pepperbush (*Clethra alnifolia*). Heavenly, honey-scented sweet pepperbush is the latest of the summer-blooming shrubs. The overall form is upright, similar to rose-of-Sharon, which I sometimes see used as a hedge; sweet pepperbush could also make a fine hedge. While most varieties are white flowered, there are pink varieties, including the attractive deep pink variety called 'Ruby Spice.' Sweet pepperbush will tolerate a fair amount of shade, especially if kept moist, but for best flowering and fragrance, give it an average to moist location in full sun.

Sweetspire (*Itea virginica*). Blooming in June, sweetspire is similar in form to the arching stems of butterfly bush and has six-inch long wands of white fragrant flowers. Unlike butterfly bush, sweetspire's autumn leaves continue to excite interest. Many showy cultivars are available, each in different shades of richly colored fall foliage.

Elderberry (*Sambucus canadensis*). While the flower form of elderberry is quite different from the preceding alternatives, the wide, almost flat umbels of elderberry sparkle in the mid- to late-summer sun. Wild ones make eye-catching displays along rural highways. Elderberries are tall, upright shrubs with attractive compound leaves. There is a particularly elegant cut-leaf variety available at better nurseries (figure 4.4). The berries make a pretty, but ephemeral, display; birds eat them even before they ripen.

Burning Bush (*Euonymus alatus*)

Yet another bird-dispersed invader, burning bush was introduced to the gardening world from Asia in the 1860s, solely on the basis of its fall leaf color. Its flowers are barely visible but do produce small berries. The

Figure 4.4. The intricate leaves of the cutleaf elderberry (*Sambucus canadensis*) are attractive long after the delicate blooms have faded.

commonwealth of Massachusetts has prohibited its sale, but it has already naturalized there and in another twenty-two eastern states. Burning bush adapts to both sun and shade and is capable of germinating in shady woodlands. Its dense foliage and root system prohibit the growth of any plant other than the hundreds of its own seedlings that germinate within its root zone. In addition to reproducing from seeds, it spreads by root suckers, forming dense thickets that crowd out natural vegetation. It is often difficult to recognize in the woods, because full sun is required to produce the flashy fall foliage.

Appropriate Alternatives

Highbush blueberry (*Vaccinium corymbosum*). People plant burning bush because they think that no other plant colors up as well in fall. They are sadly mistaken. The rich, red fall color of highbush blueberry foliage equals that of burning bush. Plus, you can eat the healthy berries fresh by the handful. Highbush blueberries have a natural upright form and can be heavily pruned for a more formal shape. If a tall shrub is not required, the lowbush blueberry (*V. angustifolium*) has equally colorful foliage. It is the same species that is cultivated en masse for gourmet blueberries in the state of

Maine and will produce equally delicious berries for the home gardener. For even more excitement, you can watch caterpillars of the Brown Elfin butterfly (*Callophrys augustinus*), eating your lowbush blueberries. Hard to believe, but sources say that the caterpillar actually eats the berries.

Winged sumac (*Rhus coppalina*) and smooth sumac (*R. glabra*). Other equally brilliant substitutes for fall foliage (but minus the blueberries) include the sumacs, both winged and smooth. Staghorn sumac (*Rhus typhina*) is equally colorful but is usually considered too tall and rangy for most garden situations (although figure 5.2 shows a cultivated tree form in England). Both winged and smooth sumacs produce cone-shaped, long-lasting, red clusters of berries in the fall that brighten the winter landscape and provide excellent bird food. The lacy-leaved (cutleaf) sumac varieties are especially attractive in all seasons.

VINES

English Ivy (*Hedera helix*)

English ivy climbs walls, is evergreen, and tolerates shade; the last two characteristics in particular have endeared it to generations of landscape designers providing that English country manor–look for their clients. Little do they realize the damage that ivy can do to walls and houses. Frequently used as a groundcover, ivy should never be used in or near a woodland, as this groundcover does not stay on the ground. Continual maintenance is required to keep trees ivy-free. This Eurasian species has thoroughly invaded eighteen states, even threatening California redwood forests. Ivy vines can reach one foot in diameter and climb as tall as one hundred feet. Ivy spreads rapidly, and its evergreen, shade-tolerant qualities spell trouble at all levels of wooded areas. As it climbs, it destroys the branches with which it comes into contact, killing trees from the bottom up, leaving them looking somewhat like giant stalks of broccoli (see figure 3.6). Ivy forms extremely dense mats on the forest floor under which no woodland ferns or flowers can survive.

Appropriate Alternatives

Woodvamp (*Decumaria barbara*). My search for an indigenous vine that remains evergreen through normal winters north of zone 7, unfortunately, has not been successful. The woodvamp comes closest, keeping evergreen leaves farther south. An indigenous member of the hydrangea family, with deep, glossy green leaves and fragrant white flowers that bloom throughout most of the summer, this climber provides southeastern gardeners with an attractive evergreen alternative for English ivy. Perhaps in the future, more cold hardy forms of woodvamp will be found that may actually keep their leaves through northeastern winters. Not surprisingly, it more closely resembles many of the related Asian climbing hydrangeas (*Hydrangea* spp. and *Schizophragma* spp.), which are also deciduous. For the time being, woodvamp can serve northeastern gardeners as an excellent alternative to the Asian climbers and may ultimately prove to be an evergreen substitute for ivy as the climate, unfortunately, continues to warm.

Additional alternative climbers. There are many fine indigenous vines that will tolerate shade, including trumpet honeysuckle (*Lonicera sempervirens*) and Virginia creeper *(Parthenocissus quinquefolia)*. One of the best is the well-named pipevine (*Aristolochia macrophylla*), with funny little pipe-shaped flowers and large, deep green, heart-shaped leaves, obviously designed to catch whatever light they can. Pipevine was used extensively to screen porches in the days before air-conditioning and is one of only three host plants, all indigenous pipevines, for the lovely Pipevine Swallowtail butterfly.

Alternative evergreen groundcovers. Although indigenous evergreen vines are in short supply, where ivy is used as a groundcover in sunny situations, several indigenous evergreen substitutes are available, including the creeping junipers (*Juniperus* spp.), such as blue rug juniper (*Juniperus horizontalis*). Common cultivars include 'Blue Rug' or 'Wiltonii' (blue-tinted female), 'Mother Lode' (with gold-tipped foliage), and 'Prince of Wales' (deep green). Creeping forms of common juniper (*Juniperus communis*), such as 'Green Carpet,' are also available. Specialty nurseries even carry a creeping form of eastern red cedar (*Juniperus virginiana*), called 'Silver Spreader.'

Bearberry (*Arctostaphylos uva-ursi*), another evergreen, is a prostrate shrub related to blueberries; it has similar leaves and flowers and produces tiny red berries. It spreads slowly and is extremely drought tolerant once established. Moss phlox (*Phlox subulata*) is a slow-spreading, herbaceous, evergreen creeper that is covered with flowers in spring.

Nonindigenous Vines and Their Indigenous Congeners

Oddly enough, some extremely invasive nonindigenous vines, still sold by nurseries, have indigenous congeners, also readily available in many nurseries. Banned from sale in Connecticut, Massachusetts, and New Hampshire, Oriental bittersweet (*Celastrus orbiculatus*), related to American bittersweet (*Celastrus scandens*), is a notorious strangler. It forms massive, trunklike vines that wrap around and pull down full-grown trees (see figure 1.4). Similarly, the two Asian wisterias, Chinese (*Wisteria sinensis*) and Japanese (*W. japonica*), related to the Kentucky (*W. macrostachya*) and American (*W. frutescens*) wisterias, also form thick, heavy vines, weighing down branches and structurally weakening trees. At the same time, the Asian wisterias' shallow roots usurp the root zone of the trees it climbs, robbing them of moisture and nutrients.

These two sets of congeners, *Celastrus* spp. and *Wisteria* spp., are practically indistinguishable, except to botanists. A telltale difference between the American and Asian species may explain one reason why the nonindigenous vines are more invasive. The indigenous vines flower and fruit at the tips of the vines, cutting off additional vegetative growth during the remaining growing season, whereas the nonindigenous vines flower and fruit at the leaf nodes, allowing vegetative growth to continue throughout the season. So not only do we have fine indigenous substitutes for nonindigenous bittersweet and wisterias, we can rest assured that our indigenous species are incapable of strangling our trees, even if we forget to prune them.

Appropriate Alternatives

For these plants, the alternatives are almost too obvious. The American wisterias are indigenous to the Southeast but hardy to zone 5, and I have had no trouble growing them in the Catskills. They can be found in both white and lavender-blue flowering forms and periodically rebloom throughout the summer. American bittersweet is indigenous to the coldest zones of the Northeast. Both male and females are needed to produce berries on this dioecious plant. The American wisterias and American bittersweet are virtually identical to their invasive relatives and are clearly better choices, from both a gardening and an environmental point of view.

Porcelainberry (*Ampelopsis brevipedunculata*)

Another highly invasive vine, porcelainberry is closely related to our indigenous grapes (*Vitis* spp.). Sold by nurseries since the 1870s for its ornamental berries, porcelainberry forms a large taproot and can spread fifteen feet in one growing season. Its dense, leafy vines cover every tree and shrub it climbs, blocking access to the life-giving sun. The results can be seen along many major highways: instead of recognizable trees and shrubs, ghostly stretches of amorphous mounds, shrouded in a single shade of green, along with an occasional dead branch sticking out. It has already spread to eighteen eastern states and is prohibited from sale in Massachusetts.

Appropriate Alternatives

Both grapes and Virginia creeper, although not congeners, as they belong to different genera, are close relatives of the invasive porcelainberry. Domesticated forms of grapes, such as 'Concord,' are good substitutes for porcelainberry, as are the wild species, if you can find a source. The delicious grapes are an added bonus. Virginia creeper (*Parthenocissus quinquefolia*) is another excellent substitute, with spectacular wine-colored fall foliage and berries for the birds.

Japanese Honeysuckle (*Lonicera japonica*)

This creeping vine has heavily scented pale yellow flowers that bloom for a short period in late spring or early summer and produce berries eaten and distributed by birds. It was introduced to gardens in 1806 for use as an ornamental groundcover and has spread throughout most of the United States. Japanese honeysuckle's semievergreen leaves enjoy a longer growing season in both spring and fall than the indigenous plants it covers, one of the reasons it is easily able to outcompete them. Spreading rapidly by rooting wherever its growing tips come into contact with soil, it destroys the natural understory or ground layer of fields and open woodlands. Birds that nest in the understory layers suffer loss of habitat when Japanese honeysuckle invades. Three New England states have banned its sale: Connecticut, Massachusetts, and New Hampshire.

Appropriate Alternatives

Everblooming honeysuckle (*Lonicera sempervirens*). Japanese honeysuckle also has an indigenous congener, everblooming or trumpet honeysuckle. It is a superior plant in all ways but one: it lacks fragrance. Perhaps because of this, it tries harder, blooming all season long with tubular, red blossoms that are such reliable hummingbird magnets that you do not even need hummingbird feeders. It also produces brilliant red berries for the other birds. Best of all, trumpet honeysuckle does not smother other plants. If the color red is unsuitable, a yellow-flowered variety of the trumpet honeysuckle can be found at better garden centers. Yet another indigenous species, yellow honeysuckle (*Lonicera flava*), with much larger yellow flowers, can sometimes be found at specialty nurseries. All are excellent alternatives to Japanese honeysuckle.

GROUNDCOVERS

Periwinkle or Myrtle (*Vinca minor and V. major*)

These innocent-looking ornamental groundcovers were introduced to gardens as early as the 1700s and have spread to thirty-nine of the lower forty-eight states. Periwinkles can adapt to sun or shade and to dry or moist conditions. They persist for decades and spread vigorously by sprawling stems that root wherever they contact bare soil. Eventually, these dense evergreen colonies cover large areas of the forest floor, even in deep shade, and outcompete and exclude delicate spring wildflowers and other natural vegetation.

Appropriate Alternatives

Golden groundsel (*Senecio obovatus*). Inexplicably the most underutilized evergreen groundcover, golden groundsel has rosettes of rounded, glossy, deep green basal leaves that last through winter. In early spring, cheerful yellow daisylike flowers rise on slender stalks about a foot above the basal rosettes to light up the landscape (color plate 11). Normally found in moist, open woodlands, golden groundsel adapts readily to ordinary garden soil and, once established, is quite drought tolerant. The basal rosettes spread slowly from seeds and shallow roots to form a continuous four- to six-inch-high groundcover. The plants are easily uprooted if they stray out of bounds.

Groundcover phloxes: moss phlox (*Phlox subulata*) and creeping phlox (*Phlox stolonifera*). These diminutive phloxes have lovely flowers, quite similar to those of periwinkle. Moss phlox is evergreen and forms low, deep green cushions that could easily be mistaken for moss when not in flower. Moss phlox loves sun and rocks and will spread slowly to drip over the edge of nearby outcrops and walls. Creeping phlox, although deciduous, is almost identical to periwinkle throughout the growing season. It is more adaptable to shade than moss phlox and thus more suitable for the woodland garden.

Additional alternatives. For sunny areas, bearberry (*Arctostaphylos uva-ursi*) and wintergreen (*Gaultheria procumbens*) are both excellent evergreen substitutes, as are the creeping junipers, covered above under the discussion of English ivy. Wintergreen requires good drainage and even moisture during establishment. In shady areas, white woodland aster (*Aster divaricatus*) has deep green, toothy leaves on sprawling stems, with bright, white daisies from late summer through October (figure 4.5). Evergreen Christmas ferns (*Polystichum acrostichoides*), Labrador violets (*Viola labradorica*), and many other indigenous woodland perennials can be used to replace periwinkle.

Goutweed (*Aegopodium podagraria*)

This persistent deciduous groundcover spreads everywhere, sun or shade, moist or dry, by both seeds and roots, and is nearly impossible to remove. Nurseries most commonly offer the form that has white-edged leaves, but it is the same plant with the same invasive qualities. Connecticut and Mas-

Figure 4.5. White woodland asters and maidenhair ferns (*Adiantum pedatum*) mix together to form a groundcover border along a stone foundation.

sachusetts have wisely forbidden the sale or distribution of goutweed. Naturalized in twenty-nine states, this Eurasian plant was already well established by 1863. An aggressive invasive, it forms dense patches that displace natural vegetation and inhibit the germination and establishment of forest trees. Unlike most invasives, goutweed is spread primarily by human introduction, by planting it in gardens and by dumping yard waste containing its seeds and/or roots into natural areas. In my own garden, I am currently experimenting to see whether a deep mulch of pine needles and/or oak leaves will smother them. I have already learned that smothering must be accompanied by consistently removing leaves that continue to poke through the mulch, usually by weed whacking.

Appropriate Alternatives

Canada anemone (*Anemone canadensis*). This low-growing member of the anemone family carpets the flowerbed with delicate, finely cleft leaves and snow white flowers that last from late May to mid-June. I have heard Canada anemone described as a "garden thug," so in an early attempt to rid my garden of the goutweed, I planted it alongside, hoping that the anemone would emerge victorious from competition between the two. Unfortunately,

Figure 4.6. The finely cleft leaves and numerous white blossoms make Canada anemone (*Anemone canadensis*) a most attractive groundcover.

neither emerged victorious, so that my efforts to control the goutweed now also force me, in many places, to remove the anemone. Unlike goutweed, the anemone pulls out readily and does not persist; it also transplants happily. Canada anemone spreads more quickly in moist conditions, but it creeps steadily uphill into dryer and shadier conditions in my garden. This urge to spread is, after all, what most gardeners seek when they plant goutweed. The fine leaves and sparkling flowers of the anemone, however, are far superior (figure 4.6).

Canada ginger (*Asarum canadense*). This is another very effective groundcover, with velvety, heart-shaped leaves rising four to six inches, and flowers like tiny little brown jugs. Canada ginger spreads slowly to form dense, drought-tolerant colonies. The leaves hold their color and form well into fall until they finally disappear, after which their shallow roots will benefit from a blanket of leaf mulch. It is best not to plant Canada ginger too close to mountain laurels and other shallow-rooted shrubs, as the two plants will compete for moisture to the detriment of both.

Other alternatives. Groundcovers can be a mixture of complementary forms and colors, rather than a monoculture. A mixture of Jacob's ladder (*Polemonium reptans*) and wild geranium (*Geranium maculatum*) can be

Figure 4.7. The Scottish garden in this photo has made excellent use of massed ferns and low shrubs in the heath family. A similar design using indigenous ferns and low shrubs such as *Potentilla fruticosa*, junipers, and lowbush blueberry (*Vaccinium angustifolium*) would provide an original, yet pleasing groundcover substitute.

quite attractive (color plate 12). Masses of spreading ferns such as ladyfern (*Athyrium felix-femina*) and New York fern (*Thelypteris noveboracensis*) make excellent groundcover substitutes (figure 4.7). And, unlike goutweed, all of the aforementioned indigenous groundcovers can be easily controlled or moved at any time should you wish to replace them with another plant.

PERENNIALS AND GRASSES

Purple loosestrife (*Lythrum salicaria*)

Purple loosestrife has overrun thousands of acres of wetlands in forty-seven out of fifty states. Its spreading roots crowd out every other plant along pond, lake, and river edges. Forming dense, homogeneous colonies, purple loosestrife reduces the amount of open water habitat for waterfowl. Four species of birds that require specialized marsh habitat avoid using stands of purple loosestrife. A population explosion of purple loosestrife plants between 1956 and 1983 at the Montezuma National Wildlife Refuge in New York State ultimately overtook 40 percent of the refuge. During the same time period, Black Terns (*Clidonias niger*) were extirpated from the refuge. Other wildlife known to have suffered the loss of habitat by the spread of purple loosestrife include Marsh Wrens (*Cistothorus palustris*) and federally endangered bog turtles (*Clemmys muhlenbergii*).

This Eurasian ornamental was introduced, probably several times, during the 1800s. Nineteen states have declared purple loosestrife to be a noxious weed. The plant has a robust, woody rootstock from which rise square stems, as many as thirty to fifty per plant, from four to ten feet tall, topped by the showy flowers. Purple loosestrife plants are long-lived. One mature plant can produce between two million and three million tiny seeds, which are blown by the wind and carried in fur and feathers miles from the source. As if this were not enough reproductive capacity, the roots of purple loosestrife spread at the rate of one foot a year.

Reports of sterile clones have been discredited. All are quite fertile and cross-pollinate readily with the naturalized species and with other cultivars. While some places, including Connecticut and Massachusetts, have banned its sale, the showy purple plants are still sold by many nurseries, sometimes by accident, as the following anecdote illustrates. When the plant appeared one summer in no less than three of my neighbors' gardens, I asked one neighbor where the plant was purchased. On visiting the local nursery she named, I was able to find a harmless perennial in a pot along with another plant, purple loosestrife, hitching a ride. The embarrassed nurseryman explained that their own grounds bordering a stream were infested with purple loosestrife and some potted perennials became contaminated with loosestrife seeds.

Appropriate Alternatives

New England aster (*Symphyotrichum novae-angliae*). Equaling purple loosestrife in height, color, and landscape impact (color plate 13), New England aster sadly is no match in a side-by-side competition. New England aster's brilliant purple-blue, gold-centered daisies can still be found beautifying swales along rural highways, but as soon as loosestrife appears alongside, its days are numbered. Although New England aster also spreads vegetatively, the more robust roots of the loosestrife, probably in combination with its capacity to produce huge amounts of seeds, means that the aster is overwhelmed within a few growing seasons. In a garden situation, New England aster does well in average soil. Shorter cultivars are available for those who do not want the plant's blossoms looking them in the eye. The flowers also come in white and shades of pink, though I still prefer the original blue.

Canada lily (*Lilium canadense*) and superb or Turk's-cap lily (*L. superbum*). Where the color purple is not the deciding factor, wild lilies make striking substitutes (color plate 14). Taller than your average lily, they branch, candelabra-fashion, extending bell-shaped (Canada) or recurved (superb) blossoms to the light. Mature individual plants may have as many as two dozen or more blossoms, creating an unbeatable floral display.

Additional alternatives. In terms of color and form, any of the numerous tall purple-flowered indigenous perennials such as blue vervain (*Verbena hastata*), fireweed (*Epilobium angustifolium*), all of the blazing stars (*Liatris* spp.), and ironweeds (*Vernonia* spp.) make excellent substitutes for purple loosestrife. Other alternative indigenous perennials, including Culver's root (*Veronicastrum virginicum*) and tall meadow rue (*Thalictrum pubescens*), add height and drama to any perennial grouping

Yellow Iris (*Iris pseudacorus*)

Yellow iris has invaded wetlands throughout the East and most of the western states. This invasive, water-loving European iris forms impenetrable stands where nothing else grows, displacing and outcompeting wetland plants. Introduced in the early1900s for ornamental water gardens, it spreads by seeds and by an aggressive, expanding root system. Although most often a problem in wetlands, it has been known to colonize upland meadows. Its roots can survive at least three months without water, and its leaves can withstand annual mowing. Connecticut, Massachusetts, and New Hampshire have banned the sale of yellow iris.

Appropriate Alternatives

Blue flag iris (*Iris versicolor*), and other indigenous irises. Blue flag, the common eastern wetland iris, is an obvious alternative. Cultivars are now available in different shades of blue and even pure white. If the color yellow is important, try one of more than a hundred varieties of Louisiana irises (*Iris × louisiana*). These are hybrids from the following five indigenous species: *Iris hexagona*, *I. fulva*, *I. giganticaerulea*, *I. brevicaulis*, and *I. nelsonii*. They come in a rainbow of colors, including yellow, as well as bicolored, complex patterns (color plate 15). Bred from natural hybrids collected from local marshes, these beauties can no longer be found in the wild. Once again, gardeners saved the day, bringing the wild hybrid irises into their gardens before wholesale destruction of the southern marshes wiped out the remaining wild populations. Louisiana irises can be grown at least as far north as Rochester, New York, where a large collection resides in the Iris Friendship Garden. These irises do not need a marsh to flourish; as long as they do not completely dry out, ordinary, moist garden soil is fine for most of them.

Miscanthus or Chinese Silvergrass (*Miscanthus sinensis*), Fountain Grass (*Pennisetum spp.*), and Pampas Grass (*Cortaderia selloana*)

Chinese silvergrass, also commonly known by its generic name, miscanthus, is an Asian ornamental grass introduced in the late 1800s that has been found to naturalize in more than twenty eastern states, plus California. Miscanthus forms dense clumps of leaves and stalks that can grow as high as twelve feet. The large clumps spread by thick rhizomes and displace natural vegetation. Flowering in the fall, the aboveground portion of the plant dies back soon after, leaving a mass of dried vegetation that is known to be extremely flammable. Tall flaming miscanthus clumps pass sparks to surrounding vegetation and fuel wildfires. Though it may spread by seeds, its aggressive root system does most of the invading. Control efforts must make sure to remove the entire root, or else the plant will simply resprout. Massachusetts has prohibited the sale of *Miscanthus sacchariflorus*, a close relative of Chinese silvergrass.

There are no indigenous fountain grasses, but the many introduced species have now found homes in every state except Alaska. These aggressive grasses form dense clumps, growing from two to three feet high. Like miscanthus, these plants create fire hazards, and worse, they are ecologically adapted to fire and reestablish quickly in burned-over areas. They produce heavy crops of wind-dispersed seeds that can remain viable for six years or more. Four species of *Pennisetum* have already been banned from sale by the commonwealth of Massachusetts.

South American pampas grass has already invaded seven eastern states, plus California and Texas. This impressive plant can reach giant proportions, with eight- to ten-foot-tall clumps and plumes as high as twelve feet. It grows rapidly, forming dense impenetrable bushes that displace natural vegetation. Its prolific plumes produce millions of fertile seeds that need no pollination and are spread far and wide by the wind.

All of these grasses are proven invaders. Virtually every species of grass, however, reproduces by wind-borne seeds; some also spread vegetatively, so the potential for invasiveness is always there. Err on the side of caution and phase out nonindigenous grasses in favor of our numerous garden-worthy indigenous grasses. These come in many heights and forms and would be more appropriate than the nonindigenous grasses used in the increasingly common "naturalistic" or "New American" landscapes.

Appropriate Alternatives

Panic grass (*Panicum virgatum*), Indian grass (*Sorghastrum nutans*), pink muhly grass (*Muhlenbergia capillaris*), and big bluestem (*Andropogon gerardii*) are good replacements for taller, upright grasses such as miscanthus and pampas grass. Many different blue- or red-toned cultivars, as well as taller and shorter varieties of Indian grass and panic grass are readily available choices (color plate 16).

Prairie dropseed (*Sporobolus heterolepis*), little bluestem (*Schizachyrium scoparius*), and purple lovegrass (*Eragrostis spectabilis*) form lower tufts with taller inflorescences (blooms), and are all good substitutes for fountain grass and other shorter nonindigenous grasses, as are the indigenous sedges (*Carex* spp.), such as oak sedge (*C. pensylvanica*), bristleleaf sedge (*C. eburnea*), and tussock sedge (*C. stricta*). There is a particularly attractive little bluestem cultivar, 'The Blues,' which has distinctive blue-tinted foliage and makes a tight formal clump. All grasses, but most particularly Indian grass, pink muhly grass, and purple lovegrass, have beautiful, glistening seed heads, especially attractive when highlighted in the late afternoon sun.

INVASIVE NONINDIGENOUS PLANTS
YOU WON'T FIND IN A NURSERY

It is useful to know about some of the invasive plants you will encounter outside the nursery as well. No nurseries, fortunately, are (knowingly) selling kudzu, also known as the vine that ate the South, or the equally infamous mile-a-minute vine (*Persicaria perfoliata*). That does not mean we can turn our back on them, especially as global warming assists their northward advance. The worst invaders vary from state to state and region to region, so it is best to check your local state conservation agency's Web site to see which ones are most likely to be found nearby. Many Web pages provide range maps and excellent color photographs of the plants in question, especially the site maintained by the Alien Plant Working Group, called Weeds Gone Wild. The federal Web site is the USDA's National Invasive Species Information Center (http://www.invasivespeciesinfo.gov), which has links to most of the local sites. Just in the past growing season, it seems, Japanese stiltgrass (*Microstegium vimineus*), a seemingly innocuous annual grass, has rapidly invaded every nook and cranny of our village. Now I have to weed it out of my garden. It is worth getting to know which ones to look out for. If you can recognize the truly aggressive ones on sight, you may be able to nip a local invasion in the bud, before it infests your own garden.

5

DESIGNING

TRADITIONAL GARDENS

WITH

INDIGENOUS PLANTS

*A familiar irony of horticulture is that
gardeners often desire plants that are
difficult to obtain.*

....

JUDITH SUMNER, *American Household Botany*

In a marvelous essay concerning authenticity in Japanese gardens, David
Slawson, renowned American designer of Japanese landscapes, states,
"Japanese garden design is not just a style of landscaping. It is an art deeply
rooted in a way of thinking and feeling about our place in nature." Though
directed to a specific style, Slawson's advice applies to all garden designers
who aspire to create works of art. There is no better way to become "deeply
rooted in ... our place in nature" than through the use of indigenous plants
in our gardens.

This chapter explores different styles and conventions to stimulate a
broader appreciation of the many ways indigenous plants can serve in the
designed landscape. For example, gardeners and designers often assume that
indigenous plants are best suited for an informal or naturalistic design.
Numerous examples, however, contradict that stereotype. The formal allée
of tulip trees at the New York Botanical Garden is one example. Rhododendrons are typical foundation plantings in suburban settings. Arborvitae
(*Thuja occidentalis*) and hemlock (*Tsuga canadensis*) frequently are used for
formal hedges.

To incorporate more indigenous plantings into today's designed landscapes, it is helpful to understand how our gardens evolved. At the risk of alienating historians of landscape design, I will use a very broad brush and simplify the field into two opposing schools: formal (or geometric) and naturalistic. For those who might enjoy the often absurd details of changing landscape fashions, there is a wonderful synopsis of Western culture's vacillation between the two extremes, which I doubt can be improved on, contained in science writer Janet Marinelli's book, *Stalking the Wild Amaranth: Gardening in the Age of Extinction.* This chapter, instead, begins with a brief history of the use of indigenous plants in American gardens before moving into design issues.

AMERICANS ABROAD

Since the earliest days of the discovery and colonization of America, newly discovered plants were exported to Europe and eagerly sought after for the gardens of scientists and royalty alike. Intrepid plant explorers trekked into unexplored parts of North America, often at great personal risk, to bring back the newest green life form for their patrons. As the colonial period picked up steam, and as the nascent nursery trade evolved, plant breeders began cross-breeding imported eastern American plants with each other and later on with new arrivals from the American West and colonies in the Far East. For example, in 1897, the French nursery Lemoine et Fils offered the first hybrid *Heuchera* to the general gardening public. Named 'Brizoides,' it was a cross between the western American coral bells (*Heuchera sanguinea*) and the eastern American purple alumroot (*H. americana* var. *hispida* f. *purpurea*).

Asters provide another example. The only two indigenous European asters, *Aster amellus* and *A. tripolium,* were valued as medicinal plants as early as 1596. The first American aster, *A. tradescantii,* was brought from Virginia to England in 1637. New England aster (*A. novae-angliae*) and New York aster (*A. novi-belgii*) were brought over in 1710, followed by smooth aster (*A. laevis*) in 1758. More species followed. Vast gardens of asters were created by collectors in England, and the exact parentage of those sold in the trade today under the name New York aster or Michaelmas daisy can no longer be precisely determined. Asters are known to cross-breed even under natural conditions. The first recognized cross, between *A. laevis* and *A. novi-belgii,* known as *A. ×versicolor,* may have formed the basis for subsequent crosses with as many as five other American species: *A. dumosus, A. cordifolius, A. ericoides, A. lateriflorus,* and *A. lanceolatus.* Asters are still very popular in Great Britain; in fact, what is arguably the largest, most complete collection of asters anywhere resides in the Wiltshire town of Devizes. Begun by a woman named Isabel Allen during the Second World War, the garden was adopted by the National Council for the Conservation of Plants and Gardens, a very good thing for the genus *Aster.*

The Europeans also developed a passion for the genus *Rhododendron.* In 1736, great laurel (*Rhododendron maximum*) was the first evergreen rhododendron introduced to England. The Catawba rhododendron (*R. catawbiense*), was introduced in 1809. In 1811, a new import from the Himalayas, *R. arboreum*, offered more color variety, and breeders throughout Europe worked hard to create cold hardy hybrids using American species. The deciduous American rhododendrons (azaleas) also attracted a great deal of interest, primarily in Belgium, after their introduction in 1738. The offspring that resulted from crosses among the northeastern American species *R. calendulaceum, R. viscosum,* and *R. nudiflorum,* and the western Asian, *R. luteum,* known as the Ghent hybrids, were so numerous and influential that the entire group was given an artificial species name: *Rhododendron gandavense.*

AMERICANS AT HOME

This brief glimpse of history points to an unlikely trend: many, if not most, of the indigenous plants commonly available in American nurseries were first commercially cultivated in Europe and returned here for sale. One of my favorite stories concerning this phenomenon appears in *Restoring American Gardens: An Encyclopedia of Heirloom American Plants, 1640–1940,* by Denise Wiles Adams (hereafter referred to as Adams's *Encyclopedia*). A prominent Iowan gardener of the late 1800s, upon hearing the news of his eastern friend's acquisition of fancy, and no doubt expensive, imported azaleas from England, could not refrain from bursting the bubble by explaining to his friend that the newly acquired, supposedly "rare" azaleas could be dug for free from nearby woods.

In researching her *Encyclopedia*, Adams meticulously analyzed trade catalogs and advertisements from the colonial period to 1940 to develop regional and national ("All-American") lists of the plants—indigenous and nonindigenous—most commonly provided by commercial sources in the United States. Numerous historical references to indigenous American plants are included, but quotations from garden designers of the times seem to indicate a common theme: Americans simply did not appreciate the ornamental attributes of indigenous plants. A close look at the "All-American" list bears that out; it contains only forty-two indigenous plants as opposed to sixty-one nonindigenous species. Indigenous trees fared well, constituting twenty-seven out of the thirty-three most popular (sadly, one of the twenty-seven, American chestnut [*Castanea dentata*], is functionally extinct), as did vines (four out of five). In all other categories (shrubs, perennials, annuals, and bulbs), indigenous plants were heavily outnumbered. Of twenty-five "All-American" perennials, only five indigenous species were included: cardinal flower (*Lobelia cardinalis*), garden phlox (*Phlox paniculata*), moss phlox (*P. subulata*), coneflower (*Echincea purpurea*), and superb or Turk's-cap lily (*Lilium superbum*). On the plus side, garden phlox was apparently the single most frequent offering, and arborvitae came in fourth overall. Appendix F lists "heirloom" indigenous plants and gives dates of early use (where documented).

The first colonists used indigenous plants extensively. Trade was limited, and survival required that any available edible, medicinal, or otherwise utilitarian plant material be put to good use. Fruiting trees and plants, both indigenous and nonindigenous, would have had the highest priority for landscaping. Trees were appreciated by early settlers for shade, sugar (maple), and the many unique and useful characteristics of different types of wood. As urban centers became more settled and prosperous, however, gardens became less about survival and more about ornamentation for its own sake (figure 5.1).

Some regions, newly settled before the turn of the twentieth century, appreciated their natural heritage more than others, often for practical reasons. Recommendations to gardeners in the midwestern and prairie states consistently mentioned a high proportion of indigenous species. As late as the 1920s, a nursery in North Dakota continued to recommend indigenous species for their superior hardiness. In more arid regions, unfortunately, then as now, gardeners resisted adopting the more practical desert landscape in favor of heavily irrigated gardens reminiscent of eastern gardens. An exception to this trend occurred in California in the early 1900s with the advent of the bungalow style of architecture and its emphasis on connecting to nature through the use of indigenous plants.

Figure 5.1. These hemlocks have been carefully sheared into formal cone shapes, a common practice that dates to colonial times.

The showiest indigenous plants have always been welcomed into American gardens. An appearance by *Rhododendron maximum* at the Massachusetts Horticultural Society exhibition in 1837 elicited astonishment from visitors who were surprised to learn that they might well trip over the same plant in the local woods. By the late 1800s, eastern gardeners showed greater awareness of the ornamental values of indigenous plants, helped along by events such as the Frederick Law Olmsted exhibit at the 1892 Chicago World's Fair. Olmsted's firm designed an American island landscape and brought in trainloads of indigenous plants; the end result was written up in an 1893 issue of *American Gardening*. It is probably no accident, however, that the enhanced American interest in indigenous plantings coincided with the turn-of-the-century English craze for "wild gardening."

American interest in gardening with indigenous plants during this period was strong enough to begin to threaten the populations of common wildflowers and ferns. This trend is only barely discernible from Adams's *Encyclopedia* for the obvious reason that people did not purchase plants from nurseries, but rather, with trowel and basket in hand, merrily helped themselves. This unsustainable practice led to the formation, in 1900, of the Boston-based Society for the Protection of Native Plants, now known as the

Figure 5.2. This staghorn sumac (*Rhus typhina*), is trained to a single trunk in an English garden.

New England Wild Flower Society, America's oldest plant conservation association. Had the society not acted, in all likelihood, formerly common plants would have become extirpated, and the rarest faced almost certain extinction. On the other hand, in accordance with the law of unintended consequences, bans on plant collection almost certainly had the effect of dampening public enthusiasm for gardening with indigenous plants. At the very least, it suddenly became a much more expensive and time-consuming hobby.

On recent trips abroad, I have amused myself (and bored my family) by photographing every American plant that I see, and I see a lot of them (figure 5.2). I have the impression on these trips, rightly or wrongly, that our plants are more popular as exotics in foreign lands than here at home. The list of plants seen is longer and more diverse than the lists of some of the American nurseries I have been to, and includes Joe-Pye weed (*Eupatorium* spp.), bleeding heart (*Dicentra eximia*), goldenrods (*Solidago* spp.), oakleaf hydrangea (*Hydrangea quercifolia*), coneflowers (*Echinacea* spp.), cardinal flower, and asters too numerous to mention. The late twentieth century saw

Figure 5.3. The foundation planting for this recently developed condominium could be located anywhere in the United States. It is characterized here by excessive use of burning bush (*Euonymus alata*) and wintergreen barberry (*Berberis julianae*). On the right, an indigenous dwarf white spruce (*Picea glavea* cv.) appears to be peeking out from behind the others.

a tidal wave of new plant (along with hitchhiking insect and pathogen) introductions from all over the globe. The jet age has broken down the natural boundaries created by the world's oceans. For plant collectors, this is a dream come true. But paradoxically, the average American yard and garden probably displays less regional diversity now than it did in the 1920s (figure 5.3). Owing to a combination of factors, including the influence of mass media, consolidation of the nursery industry, and the rise of big box mass merchandising, our private gardens have been homogenized. The same few species of plants (multiplied by their cultivars and hybrids) make up the nursery lists at Home Depot, Wal-Mart, and other chain stores all across the nation (table 5.1).

Very few of the plants commonly used today for landscaping purposes are indigenous. The practice of flooding our yards and gardens with non-indigenous plants that cannot interact with our natural landscapes is unsustainable. In years past, gardeners needed to know the qualities of the plants they grew, such as whether or not its fruits were edible, or whether or not its wood was strong enough for a given use, or whether a flower bloomed in spring or fall. It did not matter to gardeners where on earth their plants originated, just as long as they were beautiful and useful. Now we know that the

Table 5.1.

Common Landscape Plants Used Nationwide

Buxus sempervirens, common boxwood

Euonymus alatus, burning bush

Hibiscus syriacus, rose of Sharon

Malus spp., flowering crab apples

Pyrus calleryana, Callery pear

Rhododendron spp., evergreen azaleas

Rosa spp., hybrid roses

Spiraea spp., Japanese spiraea and hybrids

Syringa spp., lilacs

Taxus spp., common, Chinese, and Japanese yews

origin of a plant does matter. Recognition of this fact by garden professionals and the nursery industry is long overdue.

BASIC DESIGN CONSIDERATIONS

It seems to be in the nature of humans to impose order (at least as humans see it) on the natural world. Various anthropological theories have been proposed to explain this urge for control, which is expressed most eloquently, and pointlessly, in large expanses of mowed lawns. Somewhere in our brains, ancient survival instincts are still instructing us that nature equals chaos and humans must exercise control in order to survive (figure 5.4). All gardens lie somewhere on a continuum between chaos and control (figure 5.5). As designers, we need to recognize where in this continuum a garden should fall.

One should first ask the question: "What is the purpose of the garden, and how will it be used?" A garden can be multipurpose, of course, but it is helpful to make a list at the beginning of the design phase. Perhaps the next most basic consideration should be resources for ongoing maintenance. If you are designing your own garden, ask yourself: "How much time or money can I (or do I want to), spend maintaining it?" Most gardens designed in a more formal style will require intensive maintenance, whereas a less formalistic style will require less attention. A minimalist approach, using only

Figure 5.4. Chaos (left) vs. Control (right). These two scenes represent design extremes; most gardens fall somewhere in between.

a few carefully chosen species, may work to produce a formal landscape with somewhat reduced maintenance needs.

Good designers will find design cues from the garden's surroundings, including both the built and the natural environment. For example, a source of water is always a strong design cue. In many garden situations, the home will provide direction, particularly as to garden style. The expression of style in the garden comes from a combination of factors, including architectural features, paving, and of course, the shapes, colors, and arrangement of the plants themselves. Note that I have not mentioned plant species as a design element. As designers, let us see plants as abstract shapes, also noting size and color. If we choose our plants' shapes, sizes, and colors from our indigenous plant palette, our gardens will be part of the larger landscape, at the same time providing the visual cues needed to make us humans feel at home.

ELEMENTS OF STYLE

Each species of plant (even different individuals of the same species) has a unique combination of characteristics that determines suitability for a particular garden design or purpose. Even in the absence of pruning, some species display a dense, formal bearing, while others just as naturally form

FORMAL

INFORMAL

STYLE

ECOLOGY

MANMADE

ROCKS

HIGH MAINTENANCE

LOW MAINTENANCE

Figure 5.5. Design continuum. This series of opposing design elements empha-sizes form rather than function. When beginning a design, it is useful to have some idea of where, within the continuum of extremes, the garden should be. Illustra-tion by Michele Hertz.

Figure 5.6. This foundation planting features formal selections of indigenous evergreens: *from left,* inkberry, common juniper 'Hibernica,' and arborvitae 'Woodwardia.' At the base of the wall are individual clumps of little bluestem 'The Blues' and young azaleas.

loose, open silhouettes. Plant breeders capitalize on individual characteristics, constantly seeking out unusual plant forms for horticultural use. Certain groups of plants have received a large share of the horticulturists' attention, for example, evergreens, both broad-leaved and needled. Indigenous conifers, especially arborvitae, white pine (*Pinus strobus*), and hemlock, have proven tremendously versatile, giving the creative designer an attractive green shape and texture for every purpose (figure 5.6).

Operating on the theory that one picture is worth a thousand words, the following sections include illustrations of some common garden styles to assist a discussion of the nonindigenous plants typically used to express the elements of those styles, and examples of some of the indigenous plants best suited as alternatives because of similar physical attributes. In the illustrations, the plants are shown as numbered abstract forms. For each illustration, two lists of plants, with numbers keyed to the illustration, are provided, the first for a typical nonindigenous planting and a second list of indigenous plants to replace the nonindigenous ones in the numbered shapes. These lists are provided as examples; obviously there are many possible variations on the theme.

Tudor Style and Related Foundation Plantings

It is ironic, but probably not too surprising, that one of the most popular and attractive suburban home styles is derived from old English manor houses. Street frontage often consists of an expansive lawn, sometimes enclosed by hedges, reinforcing the British heritage style. The illustration (figure 5.7) shows a typical foundation planting, with heavy use of carefully groomed mounds of broadleaf evergreens and deciduous flowering shrubs. An asymmetrical orientation at the entrance distinguishes this style from a more formal colonial one.

Mountain laurel. This broad-leaved evergreen, in particular, has been described as North America's gift to the horticultural world. Breeders, notably Richard Jaynes of Broken Arrow Nursery in Connecticut, have greatly expanded the color range of mountain laurels, and these blindingly colorful varieties are now more widely available than the plain vanilla *Kalmia latifolia*. When used as foundation plantings, their glossy deep green leaves effectively tie the home to the surrounding landscape; they can be pruned as needed.

Catawba rhododendron. Our indigenous rhododendrons, including Catawba, were used to breed many popular hybrids such as 'PJM' rhododendrons. With large trusses of flowers, they make attractive foundation plantings or, especially in the case of great laurel, effective privacy screens. Carolina rhododendron (*Rhododendron minus*, or *carolinianum*) is the smallest of the three and could pass for an evergreen azalea. *Rhododendron catawbiense* is intermediate in habit between the other two. The *Rhododendron* species are not as readily available as the hybrids, but can be found in specialty nurseries.

Arborvitae. Another indigenous plant almost universally available at nurseries is arborvitae. It comes in an amazing variety of sizes, shapes, and colors. Plant breeders have been working overtime with this species, and at any given time, worldwide, there are hundreds of varieties of *Thuja occidentalis* in commercial production. The best of the varieties hold their formal shape, whether it be round, conical, or columnar, with minimal pruning. Colors of arborvitae range from deep green through olive and right into some lovely golds.

Figure 5.7. Tudor foundation planting. Illustration by Michele Hertz.

Typical Plants

1. *Buxus sempervirens*, common boxwood
2. *Ilex crenata* 'Helleri,' Japanese holly
3. *Rhododendron yakushimanum* 'Yaku Princess,' rhododendron
4. *Rhododendron* 'Hino Crimson,' evergreen azalea
5. *Berberis thunbergia* 'Atropurpurea,' purpleleaf barberry
6. *Juniperus chinensis* 'Hetzii Columnaris,' Chinese juniper
7. *Cercidiphyllum japonicum*, katsura tree

Alternative Plants

1. *Thuja occidentalis* 'Hetz Midget,' globe arborvitae
2. *Ilex glabra* 'Compacta,' inkberry
3. *Rhododendron catawbiense* 'Catby,' Catawba rhododendron
4. *Kalmia latifolia* 'Sarah,' mountain laurel
5. *Physocarpus opulifolius* 'Summer Wine,' common ninebark
6. *Thuja occidentalis* 'Elegantissima,' American arborvitae
7. *Cercis canadensis*, redbud

Common ninebark. The Tudor style requires a moderate amount of maintenance in terms of keeping the shrub border neatly clipped. The indigenous plants chosen as substitutes may actually reduce the amount of maintenance, as they are slow growing and hold their shape well. The one exception is the common ninebark, which sends out arching stems in similar fashion to the barberry it replaces. Unlike barberry, *Physocarpus opulifolius* has no thorns; instead it features lovely white flower clusters that bear rust-colored seed heads (see color plate 8). In this design, the compact variety 'Summer Wine' was chosen because its foliage color closely matches the purple-leaved barberry it replaces.

Inkberry. This small-leaved evergreen member of the holly family is another great foundation and hedging plant, almost indistinguishable in appearance from the nonindigenous, but more commonly planted Japanese holly and common boxwood. Readily available in most nurseries, inkberry is becoming a popular sell-out. Part of the appeal may lie in the fact that it seems to be somewhat deer-resistant, but deer will eat anything when they are hungry and, unfortunately, I have seen examples of young *Ilex glabra* completely stripped of their tiny leaves. Inkberry takes pruning very well and afterward continues to maintain its shape for long periods.

Redbud. One of our earliest flowering trees, redbud has attractive heart-shaped leaves that flush after the rosy purple flowers bloom. The shape of its leaves, height (thirty to forty feet), and overall form closely match the nonindigenous Katsura tree (*Cercidiphyllum japonicum*), which it replaces in this design. Lest you are tempted by the weeping Katsura tree, rest assured that there are weeping forms of redbud, notably 'Covey,' available as well.

Tudor style, as well as more generic foundation plantings, is one of the easiest to transition from nonindigenous to indigenous. Indigenous plants such as arborvitae and inkberry are already extensively used as foundation plantings and, as previously discussed, many of the hardier rhododendrons commonly planted are hybrids of American and Asian species. This look places a heavy reliance on broad-leaved evergreens; fortunately, the northeastern flora is well-endowed in that respect.

A Minimalist Garden Inspired by Japanese Design

In the essay referred to in the opening of this chapter, landscape architect David Slawson described the second, or "higher," of two alternative paths to design thus: "the inspiration for the design comes from within— from the desires and cultures of those who will use the garden, from the site and its surroundings (including the regional landscape), and from locally available materials." He goes on to recommend taking inspiration from

Figure 5.8. Minimalist Japanese garden. Illustration by Michele Hertz.

Typical Plants	**Alternative Plants**
1. *Rhododendron kiusianum*, evergreen	1. *Rhododendron minus* azalea 'Chattahootchee Dawn' or 'Olga Mezitt,' Carolina rhododendron
2. *Iris ensata*, Japanese water iris	2. *Iris versicolor*, blue flag iris
3. *Sagittaria japonica*, arrowhead	3. *Sagittaria graminea*, grass-leaved arrowhead
4. *Pinus thunbergii*, Japanese black pine	4. *Pinus virginiana* 'Wate's Golden,' golden Virginia pine

North American landscapes and provides suggestions for indigenous species to replace the commonly used Japanese maples, camellias (*Stewartia* spp.), and cedars (*Cryptomeria* spp.). Figure 5.8 shows a hypothetical design for a garden in a style strongly suggestive of Japanese or Chinese gardens and illustrates the ease with which indigenous plants can be used as substitutes for common Japanese plants.

Golden Virginia pine. Japanese black pine grows normally to a height of fifty feet. Virginia pine 'Wate's Golden' is a form of *Pinus virginiana* that grows slowly to maturity, somewhat less than the species maximum of forty feet. Its natural open form and the number and size of its needles closely mirror the character of the Japanese pines, even without extensive pruning. In winter, the color of its needles changes from green to gold, providing a striking landscape element exactly when it is most needed. Pitch pine (*Pinus rigida*) is another excellent substitute for nonindigenous pines but will require more pruning, unless the dwarf cultivar, 'Sherman Eddy,' is available.

Irises and arrowhead. Not only do the Japanese and the indigenous irises share similar flower size, shape, and color, but they also share cultural requirements: all need consistent moisture. Some of the more adaptable Louisiana hybrid irises can also handle ordinary moist to average garden conditions and would be perfect substitutes in a dryer location. Similarly, both species of arrowhead (*Sagittaria* spp.) are almost identical, both in appearance and requirements, with the indigenous species being somewhat taller.

Carolina rhododendron. Unlike Asian azaleas (genus *Rhododendron*), none of the eastern American azaleas (also genus *Rhododendron*) are evergreen. The Appalachian Mountains and other parts of eastern North America are rich in both deciduous azalea species (color plate 9) and evergreen rhododendron species (all genus *Rhododendron*). Because the evergreen characteristic is of greater long-term importance to the overall landscape impact than flower form, I consider the Carolina rhododendron with its small, rounded, evergreen leaves, rather than any deciduous azalea, to be the best substitute for Asian evergreen azaleas. Indigenous to the Appalachian Mountains, most Carolina rhododendrons are pink-flowered, but there is considerable variation among color and leaf size. They can withstand temperatures as low as –25°F, but some varieties may become semideciduous in the northernmost zones, especially in more exposed locations. The varieties recommended, 'Olga Mezitt' and 'Chattahootchee Dawn,' were chosen for their close approximation, in terms of habit and leaf size, to the evergreen azalea. The dwarf mountain laurels (*Kalmia latifolia* 'Elf,' 'Tinkerbell,' 'Little Linda,' 'Minuet,' and others) also make lovely substitutes for the evergreen azaleas.

Traditional Japanese gardens require a high level of maintenance. If leaves remain on moss, the moss will die. Trees and shrubs, especially, require ongoing pruning to hold their size and shape. While the use of indigenous plants certainly does not create a no-maintenance landscape, careful choices, such as the smaller rhododendron and pine used in this example, may lighten the pruning workload. In addition, the northeastern flora has a wealth of shrubs that grow to the size of small trees and exhibit naturally asymmetrical branching patterns appropriate for this style of gardening. Examples of these, as well as additional alternatives, are listed in appendix G.

Hardy Herbaceous Perennial Borders and Cottage Gardens

In combining these two garden types into one discussion, I risk offending many excellent English garden writers who maintain important distinctions among different types of historic gardens. The use of a diversity of herbaceous plant materials in confined spaces is the unifying thread in this brief discussion; I hope to irritate no one. Depending on the manner in which they are laid out, both perennial borders and cottage gardens successfully combine geometric and naturalistic elements. Varying degrees of confinement and maintenance largely determine whether the overall effect is more formal and geometric or more loose and naturalistic. Soils and moisture both play a role, as many meadow plants will be shorter and straighter in leaner, dryer substrate. Whether restrained or abandoned, the net effect of a successful perennial border at peak is a sheer riot of colors and textures.

Massed perennials confined by rigid paving and architectural elements, including the home itself, are an important, if not defining, feature of the cottage garden (figure 5.9). Perennial borders, traditionally, are larger, linear

Figure 5.9. The flowers of this exuberant English cottage garden are overflowing the walls that confine it.

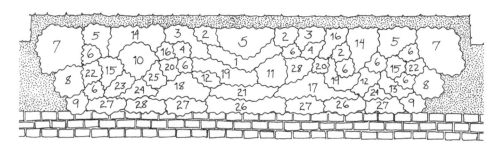

Figure 5.10. Perennial border framed by hydrangeas. Illustration by Michele Hertz.

Typical Plants

1. *Alcea rosea*, hollyhock
2. *Crambe cordifolia*, sea kale
3. *Kniphofia northiae*, torch lily
4. *Alcea rosea*, hollyhock
5. *Macleaya cordata*, plume poppy
6. *Gladiolus × hortulanus*, gladiolus
7. *Hydrangea paniculata* 'Grandiflora,' pee gee hydrangea
8. *Echinops ritro*, globe thistle
9. *Campanula medium*, Canterbury bells
10. *Paeonia lactiflora*, peony
11. *Aconitum napellus*, wolf's bane
12. *Digitalis purpurea*, foxglove
13. *Dictamnus fraxinella*, burning bush
14. *Gypsophila paniculata*, baby's breath
15. *Doronicum caucasicum*, leopard's bane
16. *Inula helenium*, elecampane
17. *Hesperis matronalis*, dame's rocket
18. *Leucanthemum × superbum* 'Becky,' Shasta daisy
19. *Doronicum caucasicum*, leopard's bane
20. *Lysimachia clethroides*, gooseneck loosestrife
21. *Allium caeruleum*, blue globe onion
22. *Agapanthus campanulatus*, African blue lily
23. *Artemisia stellariana*, dusty miller
24. *Delphinium elatum*, candle larkspur
25. *Canna × genealis*, canna lily
26. *Hemerocallis* 'Stella d'Oro,' daylily
27. *Hemerocallis* 'Stella d'Oro,' daylily
28. *Hosta* 'Bressingham Blue,' hosta

Alternative Plants

1. *Veronicastrum virginicum*, Culver's root
2. *Thalictrum pubescens*, tall meadow rue
3. *Eupatorium maculatum* 'Bartered Bride,' white Joe Pye weed
4. *Rudbeckia laciniata*, cut-leaf coneflower
5. *Eupatorium purpureum*, purple-stemmed Joe-Pye weed
6. *Sorghastrum nutans*, Indian grass
7. *Hydrangea quercifolia*, oak-leaved hydrangea
8. *Yucca filamentosa*, Adam's needle
9. *Rudbeckia triloba*, brown-eyed Susan
10. *Eupatorium perfoliatum*, boneset
11. *Baptisia australis*, wild blue indigo
12. *Monarda didyma*, beebalm
13. *Lobelia syphilitica*, blue lobelia
14. *Aster novae-angliae*, New England aster
15. *Helianthus decapetalus*, woodland sunflower
16. *Vernonia noveboracensis*, New York ironweed
17. *Phlox paniculata*, garden phlox
18. *Aster novi-belgii*, New York aster
19. *Heliopsis helianthoides*, oxeye daisy
20. *Asclepias incarnata*, red milkweed
21. *Liatris pycnostachya*, prairie blazing star
22. *Lilium canadense*, Canada lily
23. *Anaphalis margaritacea*, pearly everlasting
24. *Delphinium exaltatum*, tall larkspur
25. *Senna hebecarpa*, wild senna
26. *Tiarella cordifolia* var. *collina*, Wherry's foamflower
27. *Heuchera villosa* 'Tiramisu,' alumroot
28. *Zizia aurea*, meadow zizia

features confined between a path on one side and a wall or hedge on the other. The perennial border evolved from the large mixed border, which included roses and other shrubs, and continues to evolve in the present day, with its popularity showing no sign of decline. Many American plants were used extensively in the late-nineteenth- and early-twentieth-century garden designs of famed British plantswoman Gertrude Jekyll and, to this day, feature prominently in English cottage gardens and perennial borders. It is no very great stretch, then, to design a prototypical perennial border using only indigenous plants (figure 5.10).

Indigenous perennials. Taken as a group, generally speaking, the indigenous plants are taller and fuller with wider flower clusters than their nonindigenous counterparts. If a shorter border is required, all of the taller perennials can be cut back by a third or more in June and will still bloom in their usual season. In fact, you can stagger your blooms by leaving some and clipping others, or clipping some lower than others. The border will have a long season of bloom, beginning with wild blue indigo (*Baptisia australis*) in late May or early June, lasting right up until the asters finish in October. Unlike borders composed largely of nonindigenous perennials, which peak in midsummer, an indigenous perennial border will peak later in summer and end the season with a blaze of glory right through mid-September, maintaining occasional bright colors well into October.

Perennial or mixed borders have immense potential to eat up underutilized lawn areas, putting them back into productive use for butterflies, pollinators, and the other insects birds need for food. Perennial borders have uses limited only by your imagination; they can soften the harsh lines of a fence, or screen utilities; they can even screen your neighbors. Those who have considered meadows but have not yet taken the plunge may give the process a trial run by taking a smaller bite out of the lawn for a large perennial border, perhaps hemmed in on one side by an attractive fence with a mowed path on the other. Those of you with smaller yards and tired of mowing that patch of grass in front of your house: install a cottage garden. Trade your lawn mower (and gas and maintenance) for a red-handled pair of clippers.

A European Parterre, or Knot Garden

This style of elaborate, formal garden design came into vogue during the late Renaissance and lasted through the baroque period (figure 5.11). Herb

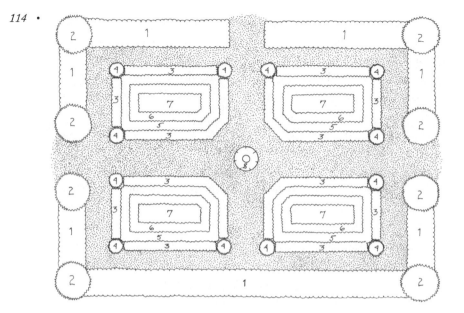

Figure 5.11. European parterre, or knot garden. Illustration by Michele Hertz.

Typical Plants

1. *Taxus baccata,* yew
2. *Cupressus sempervirens* 'Stricta,' Italian cypress
3. *Buxus sempervirens,* boxwood

4. *Pseudotsuga menziesii* 'Little Jon,' Douglas fir
5. *Lavandula angustifolia,* lavender

6. *Santolina incana nana,* lavender cotton
7. *Chamaemilum nobile,* chamomile

Alternative Plants

1. *Ilex glabra,* inkberry
2. *Thuja occidentalis* 'Degroot's Spire,' arborvitae
3. *Thuja occidentalis* 'Waterfield' or 'Amber Glow,' miniature arborvitae
4. *Picea glauca* 'Gnome,' dwarf white spruce
5. *Aster novi-belgii,* 'Rose Bonnet,' New York aster
6. *Heuchera* x 'Ruby Veil,' alumroot
7. *Phlox subulata* 'Appleblossom,' moss phlox

gardens arranged in simple interlacing patterns evolved a more complex geometry involving low, clipped shrubs and brightly colored annual flowers. The style reached its zenith (or nadir, depending on one's point of view) during the baroque period, when straight lines became swirling flourishes evoking a Turkish rug design or a garden owner's coat-of-arms. The style was imported, along with many typical plants, by colonial Americans for their herb gardens.

Inkberry. As noted previously, inkberry forms a solid evergreen foundation plant; it performs equally well as hedging material and keeps it shape after shearing. Although different from yew in texture, with tiny leaves instead of needles, as utilized in this form, the difference would be unnoticeable.

Arborvitae. The typical small boxwood hedge is replaced by a hedge of miniature arborvitae; either 'Waterfield' or 'Amber Glow' would be an excellent choice, adding another touch of color, and would require less maintenance to keep its size and shape. In a completely different incarnation, arborvitae in a tall, columnar form replaces the Italian cypress. The variety 'Smaragd' would be a typical replacement, while 'Degroot's Spire,' also a formal column in appearance, is particularly interesting, with slightly twisted, fan-shaped branches.

New York aster and purple-leaved alumroot. The sheer variety of flower and foliage colors available make the next choices difficult. Although the flowers of lavender and those of New York aster are quite different in appearance, both are equally appealing; lavender has scent to recommend it, but the aster has showier flowers. The rounded forms of the plants are of similar size and shape, although texturally different. The purple *Heuchera* was chosen for contrast, but with intense silver highlights in the foliage, it serves as an appropriate replacement for the *Santolina*.

Moss phlox. In a slight departure from tradition, the center of the parterre, usually level or slightly higher, is instead sunken, using chamomile in the first instance, with the similarly low moss phlox replacing chamomile in the indigenous design, to retain the sunken appearance. When not covered in light pink flowers, the mossy appearance and deep green color of the phlox will appear restful and provide excellent contrast when the asters bloom in fall.

While this style of gardening might well be considered the antithesis of "native plant gardening," the natural characteristics of many indigenous plants are well suited to formal patterns. And as the Christmas tree industry has proven, any evergreen can be pruned to a formal shape (see figure

Figure 5.12. Both of these conifers were found in the same nursery, pruned into the same topiary form. Either one would serve equally well in a formal design. The plant on the left is a Chinese juniper; the one on the right is a dwarf white spruce. When ecology is factored in, the spruce becomes the obvious choice.

5.12). This is a high-maintenance style of gardening, but simplicity of design and careful choice of plants that naturally maintain a tight shape can make it manageable. Additional indigenous plants listed in appendix H provide maximum formal appearance with minimal maintenance.

FUNCTIONAL DESIGN

There are many approaches to design. Leaving the stylistic concerns of the previous section aside, this section discusses different types of landscaped areas and the purposes they serve, along with suggestions for the best plants to perform those functions.

Street Trees

Trees make our streets friendlier and more inviting. Their welcome shade encourages people to get out of their cars and walk, even on hot days. With

Figure 5.13. These young street trees are 'Winter King' green hawthorns and were chosen by the homeowner for the bright red berries that attract flocks of birds in late winter and early spring.

many urban forests aging, it is time to seek underutilized indigenous species to replace the old, nonindigenous models, including, of course, the Norway maples. The root systems of all maples seem to fight against easy incorporation into urban and suburban road and sidewalk systems. Many municipalities and nurseries, unfortunately, are unwilling to bear the burden of the experimentation that needs to take place if we are to move beyond the unsustainable use of fewer than half a dozen species for our urban and suburban streetscapes. No nursery manager wants to replace a tree that fails while under guarantee, nor do any local officials want to purchase a tree that is not guaranteed and that does not survive.

Once again, proactive gardeners must come to the rescue (figure 5.13). If there is a place for a tree in front of your home, many municipalities will allow you to recommend which tree, within reason, should be planted, especially if the homeowner is willing to chip in to make the town's tree budget go a little further. Some will even let you plant your own tree. (Actually, many officials do not care whether the tree you are planting is on your side or its side of the property line; many are just happy to see a new tree planted.)

Neighborhoods can form associations to purchase and install many trees at once, often at a discount. These are all opportunities to pick one or more of our underutilized and mostly untested indigenous trees from appendix I.

Observe and record your experiment, and, if the tree does well, you will be in a position to let the nursery, not to mention friends, neighbors, and municipal officials, know what a useful tree you have found. Commonly planted indigenous street trees with a proven track record are also included in the appendix, for those less inclined to experiment.

The Front Yard

In many American suburbs, front yards of individual houses merge into an unbroken expanse of green unity. Some property lines may sport a few trees or a hedge or maybe even a line of colorful annuals, but this does not subtract from the overall effect. From our functional design perspective we need to ask what purposes the lawn is serving and how well it performs. As a symbol of social cohesion, the lawn appears to work just fine. Another common use is the lawn as sports field. If that is indeed the primary purpose of the lawn in question, perhaps a better location would be the back yard. The front yard, by definition, faces the street and passing cars, which present a danger for children and adults intent on capturing a wayward Frisbee. If the back yard is deemed too confined and the sports field must be located in front, some type of barrier, perhaps a low post-and-rail fence, might be a good precaution. Once the fence is installed, it may look a little barren without some shrubs and a few flowers to dress it up ... well, you can see where this is headed. If we make a safe and attractive sports field out of our iconic front lawn, it becomes more individual and less symbolic. Regarding lawns and fences, in some communities, putting up a deer fence is cause for shunning, yet as discussed in chapter 2, in some areas, it is becoming impossible to keep any plants without protecting them. An alternative to the lawn as icon would be some version, depending on the size of the front yard, of a cottage garden or perennial border, discussed in more detail in the previous section. In all cases, a decision must be made between competing uses, often complicated by our neighbors' expectations.

This symbol of democratic unity is a maintenance nightmare, at least if you swallow the mythology from the lawn-care industry. Ignoring this, for the past fifteen years, I have personally maintained a postage-stamp-size front lawn and a larger back yard lawn with one electric mower, no irrigation, no chemicals, and no fertilizer. Contrary to lawn-care mythology, it does not turn brown in summer. I do not mow every week or even every two

Figure 5.14. A grasshopper needs indigenous grasses and would be hard-pressed to survive on any suburban lawn.

weeks; I mow (at the highest setting) as needed, depending on rainfall and subsequent growth patterns. Our lawn does not look like a golf course, yet it is a reasonable approximation of green wall-to-wall carpeting, and it forms the perfect border for the rock garden, woodland garden, and perennial beds. This manicured greensward visually contains the wilder areas, giving the illusion of control. The contrast between the smooth, green carpet and the heavily planted garden areas is soothing and helps to create a sense of retreat. This calming influence is another job that a lawn can perform.

Now, the worst aspect of lawns, at least from the point of view of this book, is that all commercial turf grass mixes are composed of nonindigenous grasses. Very few life forms other than humans have any use for lawn grasses (figure 5.14). Buffalo grass (*Bouteloua dactyloides*) is the only grass indigenous to parts of the Northeast that forms an actual turf. While not universally suitable throughout the region, as it requires full sun and greens up later in summer than most lawn grasses, for some homeowners it may be worth an experiment. To begin to take the nonindigenous curse off my mostly shaded lawn, I have planted violets and bluets within the existing matrix of turf grasses, crabgrass, and other weeds. My latest experiments involve introducing the indigenous clump-forming Pennsylvania sedge (*Carex pensylvanica*) and hairgrass (*Deschampsia flexuosa*) to holes and edges of the lawn. Pure stands of Pennsylvania sedge have a lovely, soft, undulating quality, not quite the same effect as my green wall-to-wall carpet, but definitely better habitat.

The *New Yorker* magazine, in its July 21, 2008, issue, contained an article about Americans and their lawns by Elizabeth Kolbert, called "Turf War." In it, she states that "[r]ecently, a NASA-funded study, which used satellite data collected by the Department of Defense, determined that, including golf courses, lawns in the United States cover nearly fifty thousand square miles—an area roughly the size of New York State." We all need to do whatever we can to reduce the size of our lawns and to enhance their diversity. Happily, taking steps toward those ends will result in a livable green space that requires far less maintenance.

The Rain Garden

A rain garden can be defined as any low spot in the garden landscape to which rain water runoff from the built landscape, such as roofs, driveways, and patios, is being directed. These low spots can open up new design options for the creative gardener to use plants that require more moisture than would be found in ordinary garden soil. Rain gardens can take almost any form, depending on the shape of the landscape itself and the quantities of water that will be generated. Some are actual stormwater ponds, but most home gardens will have neither the space for a pond nor the amount of rain needed to keep a pond full of water.

Rain gardens can be as simple as a depression landscaped with a mix of water-loving trees, shrubs, grasses and perennials. If the low point of your garden is far from your house, you may want to construct a conveyance system to direct the flow to the rain garden. This can be a landscaped feature rather than an underground pipe, and it offers interesting design options. For example, our garden slopes gently from the house to the shady, and formerly dry, back yard. At first, I dug a simple trench to direct additional runoff for irrigation. Borrowing from Asian garden design traditions, the successful trench evolved into an attractive rocky stream bed. Most of the time, it remains a dry rock stream bed, with very few plants inside the actual "streamcourse" itself (figure 5.15). During storms, the water is directed downslope to my now-moist woodland garden, so that a good portion of my entire back yard is serving as a rain garden. As any gardener knows, it is much more rewarding to garden in moist shade as opposed to dry shade.

Figure 5.15. During storms, this dry stone conduit leads rainwater from the street into the woodland garden at the bottom of the slope. During droughts, a hose placed at the top of the dry streambed will water the entire garden.

With the additional moisture, I was able to introduce several new plants, including cardinal flower, Jack-in-the-pulpit (*Arisaema triphyllum*), superb lily, and swamp azalea. As a side benefit, during droughts, I can put a hose at the top of the dry stream and irrigate the entire woodland garden.

The Vegetable Garden

In the unlikely event that you should decide to plant a vegetable garden exclusively with indigenous food plants, rest assured that you will not starve. Worldwide, more than half of the crops grown are of New World origin. Recently, remains of pepo squash and sunflower seeds, dated to more than four thousand years ago, were found in archeological sites in Illinois and Tennessee. A search for a local ancestor of the squash revealed the existence in Arkansas of the Ozark wild gourd (*Cucurbita pepo* var. *ozarkana*). This plant is now considered the likely ancestor of eastern strains of domesticated pepo squash, one of the staples of Native American diets known as the three sisters; the other two are corn and beans.

Jerusalem artichoke (*Helianthus tuberosus)* despite its name, is an indigenous plant closely related to sunflowers (*H. anuus*). It produces edible underground tubers. Another tuberous plant, groundnut (*Apios americana*), though not actually domesticated, was a Native American staple adopted by the Pilgrims. Above ground, it is a vine with lovely fragrant flowers, worth having in the garden, even if you never eat the tubers. Many more indigenous fruits and vegetables are listed in table 5.2.

Whether your vegetable garden is filled with indigenous or nonindigenous vegetables, it is worth planting indigenous flowers nearby, if not actually in the garden itself (figure 5.16). You will attract far more beneficial insects and pollinators in this way. More pollinators mean increased yields from your vegetable and fruit plants. Especially with decreasing numbers of honeybees, indigenous pollinators are your best insurance policy for a fertile, productive vegetable garden and orchard. As noted in chapter 2, indigenous flowers are far more likely to attract pollinators than the nonindigenous ones.

More beneficial insects mean less damage from insect pests, such as cabbage white caterpillars, and avoiding the use of pesticides, not only in the vegetable garden but also in your home orchard, if you have one. Some fruit orchards in Russia are now routinely planted with patches of Queen Anne's lace (*Daucus carota*), milkweed (*Asclepias* spp.), and catnip (*Nepeta* sp.) to

---

Table 5.2.

Indigenous Fruits and Vegetables

Indigenous Fruits	**Indigenous Vegetables**
Amelanchier spp., juneberries	*Allium canadense*, wild garlic
Asimina triloba, pawpaw	*Apios americana*, groundnut
Diospyros virginiana, persimmon	*Cucurbita pepo*, squash
Fragaria spp., strawberries	*Helianthus anuus*, sunflower
Prunus spp., wild plums and cherries	*Helianthus tuberosa*, Jerusalem
Rubus spp., raspberries	artichoke
Sambucus canadensis, elderberry	*Phaseolus* spp., beans
Vaccinium angustifolium, lowbush blueberry	*Zea mays* subsp. *mays*, corn
Vaccinium corymbosum, highbush blueberry	
Vaccinium macrocarpon, cranberry	

Figure 5.16. Daisy fleabane and sunflower form an attractive border outside the vegetable garden fence and serve to attract many pollinators.

Table 5.3.

Plants and Plant Families That Attract Beneficial Insects

Scientific Name	Common Name	Family
Angelica atropurpurea	purple angelica	*Umbelliferae,* carrot family
Asclepias syriacus	common milkweed	*Asclepidaceae,* milkweed family
Prunus virginiana	chokecherry	*Rosaceae,* rose family
Pycnanthemum spp.	mountain mints	*Lamiaceae,* mint family
Rhus glabra	smooth sumac	*Anacardiaceae,* sumac family
Sambucus canadensis	elderberry	*Caprifoliaceae,* honeysuckle family
Solidago rugosa	rough goldenrod	*Asteraceae, aster family*

protect against fruit pests such as codling moths (*Cydia pomonella*). Here at home, indigenous plants from the same families—the umbels, milkweeds, and mints, among others—can offer similar protection (table 5.3).

The Fragrant Forest and Beyond

Here in the temperate zones, we gardeners are not quite as blessed with intoxicatingly fragrant flowers as our tropical gardening counterparts. But we are far from deprived, especially when our notion of fragrant plants includes the aromatic species, those whose leaves and twigs provide refreshing, even bracing, scent and taste sensations. If I were to plant a fragrant garden from scratch, I would use the woodland edge as a template and start with aromatic trees: white pine, yellow and sweet birch, and sassafras, together with the largest fragrant flowering trees: American linden and black locust.

Smaller trees that have fragrant flowers—the magnolias, witch hazel, hoptree, and indigenous crabapples—would be located at the wood's edge, to soak up plenty of sun for their sweet displays. Underneath these would be the aromatic spicebushes, while further out, the fragrant flowering shrubs would find space. These would include, first and foremost, the many varieties of scented azaleas, followed by sweet pepperbush, Virginia rose, and Carolina allspice. At their feet, large patches of aromatic wintergreen would bloom. Moving back underneath the taller trees, the forest floor would be planted with lightly scented woodland phlox, lemon and rose-scented trilliums, and the exquisitely fragrant trailing arbutus.

Moving out into full sun, the aromatic trees and shrubs of eastern red cedar, bayberry, and fragrant sumac would be sited, surrounded by a field of honey-scented common milkweed, garden phlox, plus aromatic beebalms, mountain mints, anise-leaved goldenrod, and sweet vernal grass. Sweet-scented fox grape would climb up and over an old snag (dead tree). At the edge of the field, a small pond would be bordered by clumps of buttonbush, sweet pepperbush, and swamp honeysuckle. Swamp pinks and ladies' tresses would be tucked in near the edge of the pond. The center of the pond would be planted with fragrant water lilies. Finally, the entrance to this imaginary landscape would be an arbor covered with Carolina jessamine, climbing rose, and groundnut.

Fragrance is a magical attribute. All of these plants and a few more, including their scientific names, are listed in appendix J. The intensity of the fragrances mentioned here varies considerably according to weather, time of day, if the plant has been pollinated, the plant's health and heredity, and the individual plant itself. Experiment with as many of these as you can. If you find a particularly fragrant specimen, you owe it to the horticultural world to find a plant breeder who will make more plants for the rest of us.

The Ever-Blooming Garden

One of the myths concerning indigenous plants that I have heard over the years concerns length of bloom. More than one gardener and designer have said to me that they would use more indigenous plants if the plants would only bloom longer. Intrigued that the comment kept recurring, I consulted a standard reference on this subject, *Gardening with Perennials Month by Month*, by Joseph Hudak. While his book certainly does not focus on indigenous perennials, a respectable minority, particularly the spring ephemerals, are included, along with a majority of Eurasian perennials. One of the "Useful Lists" at the end of the volume is titled "Perennials Blooming Six Weeks or More." Not surprisingly, to me at least, the indigenous perennials made up fully one-third of the plants on that list. Given that the ratio of indigenous to nonindigenous perennials for the book as a whole is probably on the order of one to four, northeastern indigenous plants did quite well. In fact, it is probably safe to say that most of the indigenous perennials profiled in Hudak's book wound up on the list of long-blooming plants.

I also frequently hear that there are no indigenous annuals. I think the two myths are related, because, obviously, annuals have a long season of bloom. It is one of the reasons that daisy fleabane is one of my favorite plants. My garden is lucky to have it; there are no commercial sources for it that I have been able to find. This, of course, is the reason why people think there are no indigenous annuals: most are not in commercial production. There are three indigenous annuals in common use: annual black-eyed Susan (*Rudbeckia hirta*), dotted mint (*Monarda punctata*), and Drummond's phlox *(Phlox drummondii)* (figure 5.17). All of the seeds for Drummond's phlox sold in the United States are imported from Europe, a rather sad state of affairs. Lists of some common and uncommon indigenous annuals and biennials can be found in appendix K.

The ever-blooming garden might be considered the gardener's Holy Grail. In pursuit of the grail, my gardens are a work in progress, but I will outline some of the methods that produce the best results, to date:

Group your plants, especially perennials, according to bloom times. Many spring bloomers like it a bit on the shady side, whereas many of the summer/fall bloomers want maximum sun. The ever-blooming garden needs both groups of plants, but it will be difficult to satisfy both groups in the same bed. Massed together, plants that bloom at the same time will make a better seasonal showing. To add variety, site blooming shrubs strategically to

Figure 5.17. Dotted mint, closely related to the perennial beebalms, is one of only a handful of indigenous annuals that are commercially available.

draw attention to other areas of the garden, in other words, away from the perennial beds that bloom at the same time.

Diversify your massed plantings. While it is important visually to mass similar plants together, you do not have to plant monocultures. Many closely related plants have similar foliage and staggered bloom times. The tall phloxes provide good examples. Most of us would be hard pressed at a glance to know that a mass planting of phlox actually contained three different species (*Phlox carolina*, *P. maculata*, and *P. paniculata*), not to mention twice as many cultivars. The same can be done with a shrub border; for example, the golden hypericums or St. John's wort shrubs are virtually indistinguishable from one another, and a massed planting of two or more species will provide showy yellow blooms from mid-July through September.

Use different color forms of conifers for winter interest. Nothing blooms in either of my gardens from December through the end of February, or, if it does, it is cause for alarm, not joy. Since discovering the many interesting and lovely shades of blue, gray, mauve, and gold that some conifers turn in winter, however, my pursuit of the grail has taken on added dimension. Some of the more common color varieties, such as the golden arborvitae (*Thuja occidentalis*) 'Yellow Ribbon' can be found at better nurseries. Other choice plants, such as the blue Atlantic white cedar (*Chamecyparis thyoides)* 'Yankee Blue,' may require a trip to the nearest specialty nursery. This particular conifer holds its silvery blue color year-round.

Most important, massed conifers of all colors provide excellent winter shelter for birds.

Much of this chapter has to do with exploring the limits of our comfort level: using plants that may be unfamiliar in familiar settings. We want our gardens to be refreshing and comfortable at the same time, a source of inspiration and relaxation. I hope that the information in this and other chapters will help to bridge the gap between the familiar and the strange and encourage further experimentation.

6

DESIGNS

DRAWN FROM

INDIGENOUS PLANT

COMMUNITIES

*Just as in the eighteenth century
an explosion of knowledge was balanced
by a feeling for the romantic landscape,
so does ecology fulfill a similar
function—not only because it satisfies
an emotional need but also because
we know instinctively that a lack of
appreciation of nature and our role
in it threatens life as we know it.*

....

JANET MARINELLI, *Stalking the Wild Amaranth*

In contrast to the previous one, this chapter is for those gardeners whose design sensibilities are largely influenced by natural places. We accept the notion that nature is the designer par excellence. Here I offer some general guidelines and simplified descriptions of natural plant communities or habitats to better enable gardeners to recreate them in the home landscape with indigenous plants. First, a brief word of caution; this chapter is not meant to be a text on restoration ecology. If your garden is located in a natural area and already displays many indigenous plants, you may want to consider hiring an ecological consultant or botanist to advise you. Property owners working in regulated wetlands are usually required to hire a consultant. This chapter may stimulate ideas for such areas, but is not meant to replace qualified, location-specific professional assistance.

Common Features in All of Nature's Designs

Minimal straight lines

Landscape elements appear random

Objects are well-rooted

Time and weather provide objects with a patina

Colors harmonize with one another

Few gardeners return from hiking in a natural area, be it woodland or seaside, without feeling the creative rush that comes from exposure to nature. Possibly the simplest and best advice is to find a natural area that has characteristics similar to your own property and spend as much time as possible observing the arrangement and rearrangements of the various features in the landscape. There are some common elements underlying nature's designs; the first and most obvious one is that there are few, if any, straight lines. Individual trees, rocks, and other landscape features find random placement throughout the landscape. Objects appear to be well-rooted, for example, rocks appear to emerge from beneath the earth rather than having been placed upon it. (Exceptions to the last observation are the glacial erratics, immense boulders that were actually dropped on top of the landscape by receding glaciers.) The passage of time is written on the landscape, with features exhibiting signs of weathering. Colors found in nature, even bright floral displays found in meadows, never clash; they are always in harmony with each other and the surrounding landscape. Keeping these common elements in mind will help a new garden design achieve a more natural look in a shorter amount of time.

HABITATS OR PLANT COMMUNITIES

The eastern United States rises gradually from the Atlantic Ocean to the peaks of the Appalachians, over and down into the tallgrass prairie and the Mississippi River Valley. Many different habitats, or *plant communities*, may be found within the different land forms encountered. Plant communities are groups of plants commonly found in close proximity to one another. These associations do not have rigid boundaries but rather transition gradually from one plant community to the next. Figure 6.1 portrays an

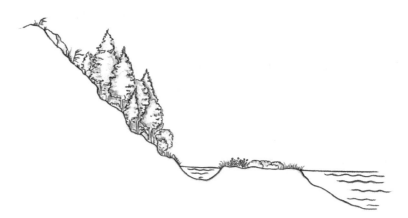

Figure 6.1. The habitat continuum, from mountains to seashore, provides the landscape context for northeastern garden designs. Illustration by Michele Hertz.

imaginary view of the Northeast from sea to mountaintop. Most of our gardens lie somewhere within this habitat continuum and provide the landscape context for garden designs. If your property is large enough, you may have room to transition from one community to another for added diversity. If your landscape is composed of varied terrain, soil, and moisture conditions, diversity may happen whether you want it to or not. It is always best, certainly from a maintenance perspective, to try to read the landscape and pick up clues as to what plant community might have originally existed rather than to impose your own personal vision, however lovely that might be.

My intention in this chapter is to help guide the process of discovering your plant community and enhancing its appearance as a garden. To that end, simplified descriptions of plant communities are provided, along with brief discussions of design issues specific to each one. For every community described, a list of some of the more common plants found there will be given. These lists are suggestions only and rely heavily on plants known to be commercially available. The organization of plant communities within this chapter follows the landscape, from the most common upland habitats, to some less common and more specialized plant communities, and ending at the seashore.

FOREST FRAGMENTS AND WOODLAND EDGE

Many scientific papers and entire books have been written about the *woodland edge* or *edge habitat* and what that means for wildlife. Suburban sprawl is currently the driving force behind the conversion of *closed-canopy forest* (essentially, large, wooded areas without openings for roads, houses, etc.) to developed areas mixed with remnant woodlands. It is by far the most common matrix within which to garden in the eastern United States. In the absence of human activity, most of the Northeast would be almost continuously forested. In ecological terms, our dwellings constitute a series of disturbances in the otherwise uninterrupted forest. Under natural (precolonial) conditions, the disturbances that opened up the forest were instead fire or hurricanes (temporary) or abandoned Native American agricultural plots and beaver ponds (slightly less temporary).

Our current settlement patterns have led to a complete reversal of this natural order, such that we now have larger and smaller forests, *forest fragments*, surrounded by the "disturbed" woodland edge. This has obvious negative consequences for many species of wildlife; however, for the gardener, it presents a tremendous opportunity. Woodland edge can be a biologically diverse and rewarding place to garden. One has the best of both worlds, a mix of sun and shade. The shadier sections of the garden will support some forest dwellers, and the sunny edge can be home to a mix of flowering shrubs and a small meadow area or perennial border. The greatest opportunity, however, comes with the use of indigenous plants; they provide the means to share our garden with other creatures and give back some of what has been lost.

The Woodland Garden

The many different plant layers in a woodland, from the overstory through the understory trees and shrubs, to the herb layer, ferns, and groundcovers, are shown in figure 6.2. If your garden is blessed with mature trees growing close enough to one another for their branches to interlock as a *woodland canopy*, you may have an area of shade deep enough for a true woodland garden, complete with spring ephemerals and other more specialized woodland plants (figure 6.3). Under an established woodland canopy, the gardener should look to add the lower layers, if they are not already present. Each one plays an important ecological role in the web of life. Depending on the size of your woodland, you may need to start moving the edge further out to accommodate understory trees and shrubs. This may involve taking out some lawn area, always a plus. It is not a good idea to plant other trees, shrubs, or even small wildflowers too close to the base

Figure 6.2. The layers of a woodland forest include overstory trees, understory trees and shrubs, and a varied ground layer with taller perennials, ferns, ephemerals, other low-growing flowers, and sedges. Illustration by Michele Hertz.

of existing large trees. Careful planting can usually be managed within gaps or at the edge of the canopy of large trees; ferns and groundcovers will migrate naturally back in toward the trunks.

If the garden is lacking adequate shade for a true woodland garden, planting a mix of quick growing but shorter-lived trees alongside slower growing, but longer-lived ones will produce results sooner than one might imagine. Under natural conditions, *pioneer trees*, which germinate and thrive in full

Figure 6.3. Spring ephemerals flower and set seed before the canopy closes in and cuts the ground layer off from most of the sun's energy. They disappear by mid-summer, but their decaying leaves provide a quick nutrient pulse to the surrounding forest. Illustration by Michele Hertz.

sun, grow rapidly, but do not live long, will come in quickly and provide the conditions for the longer-lived hardwoods and conifers to germinate and grow. Eventually, the pioneer species will be shaded out and *succeeded* by the larger hardwoods and conifers. This natural process is termed *succession* and can be used in many garden situations. Most of the understory trees and shrubs do not require full shade and so can be planted alongside the pioneer species, giving them a head start before the canopy fills in above them.

If you live near an existing woodland, some indigenous woodland plants may volunteer to come to your garden. Common ones include white woodland aster (*Aster divaricatus*), white snakeroot (*Eupatorium rugosum*), and blue-stemmed goldenrod (*Solidago caesia*). Be sure to keep an eye out for them when you weed. Do not expect to see once-common woodland plants such as trilliums (*Trillium* spp.) volunteering in your garden. Their seeds do not travel far without the assistance of either ants or humans. The limited mobility of ants is one reason most of our recovering second-growth forests lack a mature ground-layer community. Trillium and similar seeds are wrapped in delicious packages, which induce the ants to carry them off to their homes to eat, discarding the seeds onto their compost piles, where they germinate. Fortunately, horticulturists have learned a thing or two from the ants, and nursery-propagated plants are becoming more readily available. As you finalize your planting plans, remember to design pathways through your woodland and to site a comfortable bench next to the lemon-scented yellow trillium.

SUCCESSIONAL PLANT COMMUNITIES

Many people would be surprised to learn that the Northeast has a greater amount of forest cover now than it did 150 years ago. Abandoned agricultural land goes though stages; first meadow plants take over, then shrubs and pioneer trees grow into the meadow, and finally the longer-lived forest trees emerge and take over, eventually shading out all of the sun lovers. During the colonial period, forest succession was held at bay by continual intensive agricultural practices. As soon as those activities stopped, the forest began to return. Because succession is a process that occurs over time, it can be interrupted by disturbance at any point in the process, slowing or arresting the march toward forest.

Today, our main agricultural pastime is mowing the lawn. Mowing does a fine job of arresting the development of successional processes. This

Table 6.1.

The Woodland Garden

Mature Canopy Trees

Acer saccharum, sugar maple
Betula allegheniensis, yellow birch
Carya ovata, shagbark hickory
Pinus strobus, white pine
Quercus alba, white oak
Quercus rubra, northern red oak

Pioneer Trees

Amelanchier laevis, juneberry
Betula populifolia, gray birch
Populus tremuloides, aspen
Prunus serotina, black cherry

Understory Trees

Acer pensylvanicum, striped maple
Carpinus caroliniana, blue beech
Cercis canadensis, redbud
Cornus florida, flowering dogwood
Rhododendron maximum, great laurel

Shrubs

Cornus alternifolia, pagoda dogwood
Lindera benzoin, spicebush
Rhododendron periclymenoides, pinxter-
  bloom azalea
Viburnum acerifolium, maple-leaved
  viburnum
Viburnum lantanoides, hobblebush

Herb Layer

Hepatica acutiloba, liverleaf
Polygonatum biflorum, Solomon's seal
Maianthemum canadense, Canada
  mayflower
Maianthemum racemosum, false
  Solomon's seal
Sanguinaria canadensis, bloodroot
Trillium erectum, purple trillium
Trillium luteum, yellow trillium
Uvularia grandiflora, large-flowered
  bellflower
Viola blanda, sweet white violet

Ephemerals

Allium tricoccum, ramps
Claytonia carolina, Carolina spring
  beauty
Claytonia virginica, Virginia spring
  beauty
Dicentra canadensis, squirrel corn
Dicentra cucullaria, Dutchman's
  breeches
Dodecatheon meadia, shooting star
Erythronium americanum, trout lily
Mertensia virginica, Virginia bluebells

Ferns

Dryopteris carthusiana, toothed
  woodfern
Polystichum acrostichoides, Christmas
  fern
Thelypteris noveboracensis, New York
  fern

concept provides an understanding of why all of these types of communities will require periodic disturbance in the form of mowing and other more intensive maintenance than the same area of closed-canopy woodland. Within the continuum of meadow to forest, you can choose from an almost infinite variety of successional plant communities. The following descriptions are simplified examples given to provide a starting point for your own research and design. You are limited only by your imagination; there is a successional plant community to suit everyone's taste.

Meadow

For this example, let us assume that you have moved into a new house. Perhaps you do not have a lawn yet. (Maybe you don't need one.) Consider establishing a meadow on all or a portion of your property. A meadow is a diverse assembly of grasses and wildflowers working together to keep trees and shrubs out. Not consciously, of course, but the roots of the grasses and flowering plants in a mature meadow do fit together in a way that can make it difficult for woody plants to germinate and become established.

The size of your meadow and your budget will determine the ratio of meadow seed mix to plants. If you have half an acre or less, it probably makes sense to purchase at least some of your meadow plants as *plugs*, rooted baby plants that come with a couple of inches of soil. Detailed instructions for meadow establishment, from site preparation to ongoing maintenance, can be found on the Web sites of either of these two well-known meadow installation nurseries, Prairie Nursery and Prairie Moon Nursery (see appendix L), or printed in their catalogs.

Here are a few things to keep in mind as you design your meadow. Newly planted meadows must be carefully weeded during the establishment phase. The meadow will need to be mowed periodically—frequently during the initial phase, less as it matures. The meadow will not really look like a meadow until it has had at least three years to grow in. The good news is, once it has matured, it will not need to be mowed more than perhaps once every two or three years to keep trees and shrubs out; many, however, mow their meadows every year, usually in late winter. Unless you are in a rural area, your meadow will need to be visually contained, which can be done simply by mowing a strip around the edges (figure 6.4).

Consider the transition of meadow to house. If you lay out a system of

Figure 6.4. The mowed edge at the top of this meadow adds definition.

paths in advance, you can save money and time on seeds, plants, and maintenance. The seeds of many wildflowers are quite expensive. It may make more sense to buy a few of the more expensive ones as plants, rather than seeds, install them in the meadow, and hope that they will self-sow. It does complicate the mowing routine during establishment to have small plants interspersed within seeded areas; weed whackers are useful in this situation. Placing the small plants together in groups alleviates the mowing issue somewhat and usually looks much better from a design perspective. You will still need to put down meadow seed in the planted area to avoid a patchy look once the meadow grows in. You may want to limit the seeds in those areas to grasses only, assuming you have planted flowering plants.

A good way to transition from house to meadow, and add more seeds to your meadow at the same time, is to plant a perennial or mixed border near the house. Perennial borders are really nothing more than elegantly planned, carefully contained mini-meadows with maximum flower power and fewer grasses. Most of the perennials used in a border will happily make themselves at home wherever their seeds can find a bare patch. You can also clip off the mature seed heads in fall and lay them down in the meadow. Your perennial border will provide a sneak preview of what your meadow will look like, albeit with fewer grasses. This brings up the evolutionary method of meadow creation. You can start with one or more mini-meadows and simply keep enlarging them until you reach the meadow of your dreams. This evolutionary method can be quite useful in the more dense suburban areas where everyone's yard is subject to neighborly inspection.

Your meadow will be most successful if you understand the characteristics of your soil. Some plants will perform better in sandy loam, others better in wet clay. If there are any examples of natural meadows nearby, even an overgrown pasture, check to see what types of indigenous plants are growing there. On drier sites, you will probably see more grasses and fewer wildflowers. Overall, the vegetation on drier sites will usually not be as tall. Moister sites will produce the tallest, showiest flowering meadows. They can also be more difficult to maintain, because everything wants to grow there. Naturally growing moist meadows often provide spectacular roadside shows, with the tall purple and rose heads of ironweed and Joe-Pye weed waving in the breeze. Understanding your site in relation to its surroundings will produce the most natural-looking result.

Choose a diversity of plants, as many different ones as the budget will allow, for the reason that once the meadow has grown in, it is difficult, if not impossible, to add new meadow plants. Subtraction is much easier. Do not neglect the grasses. They are truly the foundation of your meadow and will rescue it in times of drought. A healthy dose of grasses can keep taller perennials from flopping if it turns out that your site has more moisture than you thought it had. Grasses will form a more resilient matrix, bouncing back after inclement weather. They also extend the magical season well into late fall, when golden seed heads catch the light, and add structural interest in winter. As a general rule of thumb, I use more little bluestem and side-oats grama on the higher, drier sites, and big bluestem, panic grass, and Indian grass on the moister, heavier soils.

Careful attention to flowering times can provide color from early summer on, beginning with tall meadow rue and beebalm. It is too much to expect that plants that will grow three, four, or more feet tall before blooming could be ready to flower in springtime. Smaller, spring flowering plants would likely not persist in a typical moist meadow, although they can be useful in the start-up phase and may survive in a drier, shortgrass prairie. A cluster of blue flag, copper, or Louisiana irises (*Iris* spp.) can add a touch of early season color at the edge of a wet meadow. These should not be sprinkled throughout, but rather grouped together for aesthetic, cultural, and maintenance reasons. Their swordlike leaf blades are too distinctive to mix well, and their thick rhizomes keep most other plants away. It is also a good idea to plant some spring-flowering shrubs at the edges of the meadow. Make sure that any shrubs you choose to plant alongside a meadow do not spread by runners. Red-osier dogwood (formerly known, with good reason,

Table 6.2.

Meadow

Wildflowers

Agastache scrophulariifolia, giant purple hyssop

Allium cernuum, nodding pink onion

Angelica atropurpurea, angelica

Asclepias incarnata, swamp milkweed

Aster laevis, smooth blue aster

Aster novae-angliae, New England aster

Aster pilosus, frost aster

Cassia (Chamaechrista) fasciculata, partridge pea

Coreopsis lanceolata, tickseed

Dalea (Petalostemum) purpurea, purple prairie clover

Eupatorium maculatum, Joe-Pye weed

Eupatorium perfoliatum, boneset

Gaura biennis, biennial beeblossom

Heliopsis helianthoides, tall sunflower

Lobelia syphilitica, blue lobelia

Monarda spp., beebalms

Penstemon digitalis, white beardtongue

Phlox maculata, wild sweet William

Physostegia virginiana, obedient plant

Pycnanthemum pilosum, hairy mountain mint

Rudbeckia fulgida, orange coneflower

Rudbeckia hirta, black-eyed Susan

Rudbeckia triloba, brown-eyed Susan

Senna hebecarpa, tall cassia

Solidago speciosa, showy goldenrod

Thalictrum pubescens, tall meadow rue

Verbena hastata, blue vervain

Vernonia noveboracensis, New York ironweed

Veronicastrum virginicum, Culver's root

Zizia aurea, golden Alexanders

Grasses

Andropogon gerardii, big bluestem

Bouteloua curtipendula, side-oats grama

Elymus canadensis, Canada wild rye

Panicum virgatum, switchgrass

Schizachyrium scoparium, little bluestem

Sorghastrum nutans, Indian grass

as *Cornus stolonifera*, now known as *Cornus sericea* subsp. *sericea*), for example, would be a very poor choice.

Do not expect much from your meadow during the first year or two. The first order of business for meadow plants is to put down deep, healthy roots. During this time, plants ration the energy they allow for top growth. Only your annuals will flower the first year. Your patience, however, will be amply rewarded when, during the third growing season, the meadow really begins to come together. Thereafter, the parade of seasonal floral displays will

Figure 6.5. This sandplain grassland, or low meadow, is dominated by blue-eyed grass, wild strawberries, and dwarf cinquefoil in spring; by late summer grasses will have grown no higher than eighteen inches.

increase and intensify at the same time your maintenance duties decrease. Not that you will want to spend less time in the meadow; but you will be able to switch your emphasis from weeding to butterfly watching.

Sandplain Grassland

If you have an extremely well-drained, sunny site and your soils are on the sandy side of loam, you may want to try to establish a low meadow, known as shortgrass prairie, or sandplain grassland. These specialized plant communities are quite rare, and will not persist unless the soil conditions are just right. It is not uncommon in many parts of the Northeast to find areas of soil that appear to be sand piles dumped off the back of a pickup truck. They were, in fact, dumped by a receding glacier. Perhaps you have been wondering about that scrubby area out back that never seems to grow much except a few scraggly grasses and clumps of goldenrod. If, in fact, you are blessed with glacial deposits, you may want to take advantage of the opportunity to create a low, xeric meadow, a garden ver-

Table 6.3.

Sandplain Grassland

Wildflowers

Anaphalis margaritacea, pearly everlasting	*Liatris scariosa* var. *novae-angliae*, northern blazing star
Antennaria neglecta, pussytoes	*Lupinus perennis*, eastern lupine
Asclepias tuberosa, orange milkweed	*Monarda fistulosa*, wild bergamot
Aster ericoides, many-flowered aster	*Monarda punctata*, spotted beebalm
Aster linarifolius, stiff aster	*Potentilla canadensis*, dwarf cinquefoil
Aster pilosus, heath aster	*Rudbeckia hirta*, black-eyed Susan
Baptisia tinctoria, wild yellow indigo	*Sisyrinchium* spp., blue-eyed grasses
Dodecatheon meadia, shooting star	*Solidago nemoralis*, gray goldenrod
Erigeron pulchellus, robin's plantain	*Solidago puberula*, downy goldenrod
Fragaria virginiana, wild strawberry	*Tephrosia virginiana*, goat's rue
Geum triflorum, prairie smoke	*Viola fimbriatula*, ovate-leaved violet
Hedyotis caerulea, bluet	*Viola pedata*, bird's-foot violet
Hypoxis hirsuta, yellow star grass	

Grasses

Bouteloua curtipendula, side-oats grama	*Eragrostis spectabilis*, purple lovegrass
Danthonia spicata, poverty grass	*Schizachyrium scoparium*, little bluestem

sion of a sandplain grassland (figure 6.5). Even more common in the Northeast, the lovely little bluestem grass still forms almost pure stands along roadsides and other sandy barrens where trees have not been able to reassert their dominance. As roadside vegetation becomes increasingly overtaken by nonindigenous invaders, these natural communities will not be with us much longer.

Carefully executed, you could provide a rare habitat for specialized plants and animals. Even the common painted turtle favors sandy areas to dig a nest and lay eggs. Unlike a moist meadow, you can mix diminutive spring-bloomers such as pussytoes, blue-eyed grass, bird's-foot violet, and shooting star, with yellow baptisia, butterfly weed, prairie smoke, and the signature northeastern prairie plant, eastern lupine. These specialized plants would almost certainly be overwhelmed in a typical moist meadow. Before adding new plants, however, it is a good idea to inventory what you already have. If

Figure 6.6. A typical old field in the process of becoming forest again as the trees on the right move farther out into the open, shading the highbush blueberries and meadow flowers.

it has not been completely overrun by invasive plants, you may find a few indigenous treasures.

Old Field

If you are establishing a brand-new garden in a brand-new subdivision, this might be the habitat to aim for, at least in the short term. In fact, if you did nothing but let nature take its course, in a few years, an old field is what you might wind up with. An old field is the next phase of the continuum from meadow to forest. The elements of an old field include grasses, wildflowers, shrubs, and pioneer trees. Figure 6.6 is a photograph of an old field in the Catskill Mountains now dominated by highbush blueberries. This old field is bordered on the right by a woodland edge. If one were to mow a wide enough path through the wildflowers down the center past the large blueberry, you could have a perfectly acceptable garden. Some lucky folks have actually bought old farms and can pretty much do just that (figure 6.7).

Assume, as in the previous example, you are working with a much cleaner slate. Begin with a meadow; however, you will need to incorporate *woody* plants, perhaps one pioneer tree and some shrubs, into your meadow design.

Figure 6.7. This old field has been carefully cultivated, arresting the progress of succession through the simple act of mowing paths and thus grooming this natural landscape as a lovely garden.

(You could also plant your meadow, and after it is established, just stop mowing, stand back, and watch what happens.) Personal aesthetics will largely determine the ratio of meadow to woody plants, as well as the complexity and diversity of the plants chosen. It is possible in nature to find examples of old fields that are incredibly diverse as well as examples that are dominated by only a few species. Fields of eastern red cedars and meadow flowers and not much else can be quite attractive. Highbush blueberry fields are another common example and turn shades of brilliant scarlet and plum in the fall.

The more woody plants you bring in, the more complicated the mowing becomes. To achieve a natural look, the trees and shrubs will require random placement. As it is virtually impossible for humans to create "randomness," we resort to tricks. One way is to pick up a handful of stones and throw them out into the field. Plant the shrubs or trees where the rocks fall. Another trick, if weeds have already gotten a head start, is to pick a few of the largest ones, dig them out and plant your shrubs in their place. Unlike humans, weeds have a great sense of randomness. If you are planting more than one of the same species (which is usually a better idea than one each of many different species), be sure to purchase different-size plants for a more natural appearance. As you put the finishing touches on your design, remember to site a path to the biggest blueberry bush.

Table 6.4.

Old Field

Pioneer Trees	Shrubs
Amelanchier arborea, serviceberry	*Cornus racemosa,* gray dogwood
Betula populifolia, gray birch	*Prunus virginiana,* chokecherry
Juniperus virginiana, eastern red cedar	*Sambucus canadensis,* elderberry
Populus grandidentatum, big-toothed aspen	*Vaccinium corymbosum,* highbush blueberry
Prunus pensylvanicus, pin cherry	*Viburnum dentatum,* arrowwood

Fern Glade

A variation on the typical meadow or old field is a fern glade. Taller clumped ferns such as cinnamon fern surrounded by lower spreading ferns, such as New York, lady, or hay-scented, shaded by deciduous trees, especially birches, are a signature landscape of the Great North Woods (figure 6.8). Essentially, ferns replace grasses and wildflowers as the dominant herbaceous groundcover; in some cases, the taller ferns can actually replace the shrub layer, at least visually. If your soil is naturally moist, or if you already have existing mature trees casting abundant shade, it may be possible to establish large areas of ferns as groundcover. In the absence of existing large trees, adding attractive pioneer species, such as willows or birches, will complete the scene. You will want to include some spring ephemerals to provide spring color and texture before the ferns unfurl their fronds in late spring. Natural fern glades can be surprisingly resistant to succession. Some foresters believe that hay-scented ferns, in particular, form a monoculture and release chemicals that inhibit tree germination. While fern glades lack the summer flower display, they can provide soothing, serene refuges from the everyday world.

Figure 6.8. Fern glade. This moist, second-growth woodland supports a thriving ground layer of New York ferns and a taller level of cinnamon ferns, shaded by the filtered light of gray birches.

Table 6.5.
Fern Glade

Pioneer Trees and Tall Shrubs

Betula nigra, river birch
Betula papyrifera, paperbark birch
Betula populifolia, gray birch
Carpinus caroliniana, blue beech
Cornus alternifolia, pagoda dogwood
Hamamelis virginiana, witch hazel
Lindera benzoin, spicebush

Taller Ferns

Dryopteris goldiana, Goldie's fern
Osmunda cinnamomea, cinnamon fern
Osmunda claytoniana, interrupted fern

Evergreen Ferns for Accent

Dryopteris intermedia, evergreen
    woodfern
Polystichum acrostichoides, Christmas
    fern

Ferns That Form a Groundcover

Athyrium filix-femina, lady fern
Dennstaedtia punctilobula, hay-scented
    fern (best for drier sites)
Thelypteris noveboracensis, New York
    fern

Blueberry Heath

A *heath* is a plant community composed primarily of dwarf shrubs (many of which happen to be members of the heath plant family). These special places usually occur on sandy acid soils of low fertility. The most common heaths in the Northeast are those dominated by lowbush blueberries. For those who love miniature landscapes, nothing comes closer to a dwarf version of an old field than a blueberry heath, except that the low, nearly uniform size of the plants provides a tidier appearance (figure 6.9). Many heaths come complete with what appear to be miniature conifer forests, but are, in fact, club mosses (*Lycopodium* spp.). The low-growing, spreading forms of our indigenous heath plants in an open setting often appear to be maintained by an unseen hand.

The most common of the lowbush blueberry–type plants is *Vaccinium angustifolium*, but there are others with such similar leaves, berries, and flowers that they are difficult to tell apart (figure 6.10). Even black huckleberry, the tallest at two to three feet, looks quite similar. The blueberries grow together forming large patches (clonal patches may be circular) separated by

Figure 6.9. Blueberry heath. This photo shows dark patches of lowbush blueberries, surrounded by poverty grass and club mosses. Despite the impoverished nature of the soil, the forest will gradually creep back in—absent fire, mowing, or other disturbance.

Figure 6.10. Flowers of the lowbush blueberry (*Vaccinium angustifolium*) are often described as urn-shaped.

Table 6.6.

Blueberry Heath

Trees and Taller Shrubs

Betula populifolia, gray birch

Juniperus virginiana, eastern red cedar

Kalmia latifolia, mountain laurel

Vaccinium corymbosum, highbush
   blueberry

Grasses and Groundcovers

Danthonia spicata, poverty grass

Deschampsia flexuosa, common hairgrass

Epigaea repens, trailing arbutus

Gaultheria procumbens, wintergreen

Rubus hispidus, dewberry

Low Shrubs

Arctostaphylos uva-ursi, bearberry

Gaylussacia baccata, black huckleberry

Kalmia angustifolia, sheep laurel

Rosa carolina, Carolina rose

Vaccinium angustifolium, lowbush
   blueberry

Vaccinium myrtilloides, velvetleaf
   huckleberry

Vaccinium pallidum, early low
   blueberry

Vaccinium vacillans, dry-land blueberry

poverty or other grass and low-growing wildflowers and ferns. It can be visually effective to frame the open areas of low shrubs with slow-growing trees and taller shrubs, such as mountain laurel. Successional blueberry heaths are naturally fire-adapted; in the absence of fire, the forest will slowly overtake the low shrubs, despite the poor soil. Unlike many trees, blueberries sprout back rapidly from strong root systems after fire. Where fire is deemed too dangerous, mowing can take its place.

Savannahs and Oak Openings

Sometimes succession is arrested naturally by limitations in the soil depth, such as underlying bedrock, soil moisture conditions, or a combination of both. Such physical characteristics create open areas sparsely populated by trees surrounded by grassy meadows. A plant community once common in the Midwest, the oak savannah, unfortunately, has been almost wiped out. Here in the Northeast, the term *oak openings* is used to describe a similar natural community now usually limited to higher elevations and also increasingly rare (figure 6.11).

Figure 6.11. This oak forest covers the shallow soils of a dry, rocky ridge. These conditions lead to naturally stunted growth in the trees, as well as the open, park-like nature of the canopy and ground layer.

Table 6.7.

Savannahs and Oak Openings

Trees	Grasses
Carya alba (tomentosa), mockernut hickory	*Andropogon gerardii*, big bluestem
Quercus alba, white oak	*Schizachyrium scoparium*, little bluestem
Quercus coccinea, scarlet oak	*Sorghastrum nutans*, Indian grass
Quercus muhlenbergii, chinquapin oak	
Quercus prinus, chestnut oak	

It might surprise some to learn that the typical American lawn dotted with specimen trees would be viewed as a type of savannah, robbed, however, of ecological content, purpose, and context. It is interesting to imagine how simple it would be to begin putting the landscape back together by tweaking America's dominant landscape model in a more positive direction. One could begin by replacing the Norway maple and any other nonindigenous shade trees with oaks and other indigenous trees. Replace the lawn with buffalo grass (*Bouteloua dactyloides*), low-growing sedges, or carpets of violets, all of which can be mowed. It could easily be done; repeated on thousands of properties, the result would be transformational.

For those interested in a more diverse savannah, one that could mimic examples found under natural conditions, a wider choice of plants would be used. In addition to oaks and other indigenous trees, the clonal shrub, gray dogwood (*Cornus foemina* subsp. *racemosa*), is commonly found in oak openings. For the grassy meadow ground layer, the taller wildflowers listed under sandplain grassland would provide a good start.

Rock Ledge

If your home is situated on a rock ledge, you are fortunate indeed. Rocks are beautiful in their own right. They are low maintenance and do not need to be mowed. Continuous rock formations covered by a thin layer of soil will make their presence known. The use of ivy, grass, periwinkle, and other nonindigenous plants to disguise rocks as part of the lawn is inexplicable. It simply creates more work for the homeowner. Peel back those ancient layers of

Figure 6.12. This artificial rock formation in the Catskills has been planted with the Catawba rhododendron 'Roan Mountain' from the Appalachians. Other plants include eastern red cedar on the left and the evergreen groundcover *Potentilla tridentata*.

vines and detritus once and for all. Expose your rocks proudly. Allow them to become encrusted with low-maintenance lichens.

Natural communities that you can emulate include rocky summits known in some areas as *balds*. Rocky summits are closely related to the oak openings and other sparsely wooded hill and ridge-top plant communities and may be interspersed with or found alongside them. Balds found in the Appalachian mountain highlands are some of the most colorful flowering landscapes in the world when the azaleas, rhododendrons, and laurels are in bloom. The summits are covered with several *Rhododendron* species in a rainbow of colors that mix and match, hybridizing freely, some believe, since the glaciers receded. Further north, relict boreal landscapes with rare dwarf plants persist on mountaintops in New York's Adirondacks and Shawangunks, as well as in the White Mountains of New Hampshire.

While some of these plants are too specialized for the average garden, many adapt to a wide range of conditions and are found in other plant communities—for example, the azaleas, rhododendrons, lowbush blueberry, and bearberry (figure 6.12). Specialty nurseries can provide many natural hybrid azalea and rhododendron species. Since the 1950s, roots, cuttings, seeds, and

Figure 6.13. Plants tucked into crevices of the rock ledge include creeping juniper, columbine, bleeding heart, *Sedum ternatum,* bluets, and ferns.

pollen from the most beautiful and unusual azaleas and rhododendrons of Appalachian balds have been carefully collected and propagated by plant breeders (color plate 9) and are ready for today's gardeners to enjoy, whether you are gardening high or low, with or without rock. Most are cold hardy, as they are genetically acclimated to alpine conditions.

Creating an indigenous plant community that resembles a rock ledge or bald is not so very different from creating any other type of alpine or rock garden, with three exceptions: first, use of indigenous plants; second, use of existing substrate; and third, making the rocks and their lichen associates just as important as the flowers (figure 6.13). Some fortunate alpine gardeners do have a natural rock substrate to work with, but many other enthusiasts are forced to create their own on a much smaller scale.

As with any other natural design project, it is important to find local examples to use as models. You can still incorporate into your design that gorgeous azalea from North Carolina that you just saw at the specialty nursery, but by making sure most of your plants are locally adapted, your chances of success will increase, and your garden will look as if it belongs with the surrounding landscape. Where I live, much of our village sits on an immense rock ledge overlooking the Hudson River. A large, natural area park still supports a rare community of plants adapted to hanging off rocks, supported only by thin, xeric soils (figure 6.14). Some local gardeners choose to work

Figure 6.14. This natural rock ledge has wild pinks (*Silene caroliniana*), wild lettuce (*Lactuca* sp.), and grasses growing in the cracks.

with the ledge; perhaps they are inspired by the local park. Others have allowed the rocks to become obscured by ivy and other groundcovers, certainly a missed design opportunity. Where visible, the rock ledge adds greatly to local visual character.

FRESHWATER STREAMS, PONDS, AND OTHER WETLANDS

Local topography will determine whether the water feature closest to your garden is a relatively narrow, swift-flowing stream, a wider stream surrounded by a level floodplain, or a series of ponds or lakes. Slow-moving, meandering streams are usually bordered by wide, flat floodplains and a correspondingly greater variety of plant communities. Floodplain forests, shrub swamps, marshes, and wet meadows can all be found alongside, depending on soils and topography. These plant communities share many similarities with those found at the edges of lakes and ponds. In simplest terms, a marsh is a very wet meadow, a swamp is a very wet savannah, and a bog is a floating heath with cranberries substituting for blueberries. The unifying feature in all of these is, of course, a requirement for more moisture than is found in ordinary garden soil. That does not mean that it is impossible to incorporate

Table 6.8.

Rock Ledge

Dwarf Trees

Abies balsamea 'Nana,' dwarf balsam fir

Betula nana, dwarf birch (or substitute *Betula nigra* 'Little King,' dwarf river birch)

Picea glauca 'Echiniformis,' dwarf white spruce

Picea mariana 'Nana,' dwarf black spruce

Quercus ilicifolia, bear oak

Azaleas and Rhododendrons

Rhododendron arborescens, sweet azalea

Rhododendron catawbiense 'Roan Mountain,' Catawba rhododendron

Rhododendron cumberlandense, Cumberland azalea

Rhododendron minus, Carolina rhododendron

Rhododendron × 'Gregory Bald' (*R. calendulaceum* hybrid), hybrid azalea

Rhododendron × 'Wayah Crest' (*R. arborescens* × *R. cumberlandense*), hybrid azalea

Low Shrubs

Arctostaphylos uva-ursi, bearberry

Corema conradii, broom crowberry

Empetrum nigrum, black crowberry

Leiophyllum buxifolium, sand myrtle

Paxistima canbyi, Canby's mountain-lover

Vaccinium angustifolium, lowbush blueberry

Vaccinium caespitosum, dwarf bilberry

Vaccinium vitis-idaea subsp. *minus*, northern mountain cranberry

Perennials

Aquilegia canadensis, rock bells

Aster linariifolius, pine-leaved aster

Campanula rotundifolia, harebell

Chrysogonum virginianum, green and gold

Conradina verticillata, Cumberland rosemary

Delphinium tricorne, spring larkspur

Dodecatheon meadia, shooting star

Draba arabisans, rock cress

Epigaea repens, trailing arbutus

Erythronium americanum, trout lily

Hexastylis shuttleworthii, mottled wild ginger

Houstonia caerulea, bluet

Hypoxis hirsuta, yellow stargrass

Opuntia humifusa, prickly pear cactus

Phlox subulata, moss phlox

Sedum ternatum, woodland stonecrop

Sibbaldiopsis (Potentilla) tridentata, three-toothed cinquefoil

Silene caroliniana var. *pensylvanica*, wild pink

Solidago multiradiata var. *arctica* (*S. cutleri*), alpine goldenrod

Trillium nivale, snow trillium

Table 6.8., cont.

Rock Ledge

Ferns and Grasses

Asplenium trichomanes, maidenhair spleenwort

Carex pensylvanica, Pennsylvania sedge

Deschampsia flexuosa, common hairgrass

Polypodium virginianum, common rock polypody

Polystichum braunii, Braun's hollyfern

Woodsia alpina, alpine woodsia

Woodsia ilvensis, rusty woodsia

some of these plants into the garden. It does mean that a full assemblage of these plants as a community will require a consistent source of water, either natural or constructed.

Marsh

Perhaps you are planning to create a stream as part of a recirculating pond system; if so, you will need to decide where, between the extremes of rocky headwater and meandering floodplain, your ideal stream will fall. Working with your existing terrain will be most cost-effective and will provide the most natural-looking result. In a swiftly moving stream, the placement of rocks is as important as the placement of plants. Plants most likely to be successful along a steep, rocky stream are large trees with strong root systems. Leaf litter and insect larvae from indigenous trees planted along the banks will contribute to the riverine food web. The trees will also shade the stream, keeping water temperatures cool enough for coldwater fishes such as trout to survive in the hot summer months (figure 6.15).

A newly created stream will require a variety of rocks, riffles (with a waterfall, of course), and pools of quiet water in order for it to look natural. It is possible to tuck marsh plants into rocky crevices along the running portion of the stream, but a marsh community requires a relatively quiet, undisturbed pond (probably not the same one your waterfall splashes into, unless it is quite large), either at the beginning or end of the stream. If there is an existing pond, you can begin to design the marsh according to the existing

Figure 6.15. A swift-moving headwater stream is hemmed in on either side by a healthy riparian forest. Leaf litter and insect larvae from these trees contribute to the riverine food web.

Figure 6.16. An old farm pond has been dressed up with water lilies, Joe-Pye weed, blue flag iris, arrowhead, and a fast-growing black willow at the edge.

Table 6.9.

Freshwater Marsh

Shrubs

Cephalanthus occidentalis, buttonbush

Clethra alnifolia, sweet pepperbush

Ilex verticillata, winterberry

Rhododendron viscosum, swamp honeysuckle

Salix discolor, pussy willow

Salix nigra, black willow

Salix sericea, silky willow

Sambucus canadensis, elderberry

Spiraea tomentosa, steeplebush

Wildflowers and Sedges

Acorus americanus, sweet flag

Asclepias incarnata, swamp milkweed

Boltonia asteroides, false aster

Calla palustris, wild calla lily

Caltha palustris, marsh marigold

Carex stricta, tussock sedge

Chelone glabra, turtlehead

Eleocharis palustris, common spikerush

Eupatorium maculatum, spotted Joe-Pye weed

Eupatorium perfoliatum, boneset

Helenium autumnale, Helen's flower

Iris versicolor, blue flag iris

Juncus effusus, soft rush

Lilium canadense, Canada lily

Lobelia cardinalis, cardinal flower

Pontederia cordata, pickerelweed

Sagittaria graminea, grass-leaved arrowhead

Saururus cernuus, lizard's tail

Scirpus cyperinus, woolgrass

Thalictrum pubescens, tall meadow rue

Verbena hastata, blue vervain

Ferns

Onoclea sensibilis, sensitive fern

Thelypteris palustris, marsh fern

Aquatic Plants

Nuphar advena, yellow pond lily

Nuphar variegata, spatterdock

Nymphaea odorata, fragrant water lily

water levels. If it is to be a new pond, the marsh should dictate the design of the pond's edge in order to accommodate a diversity of plant species. Marsh plants are categorized according to the depth of water they will tolerate. Aquatic plants, such as water lilies, for example, require a foot or more of water throughout the growing season for best results, and should be placed in the deepest section of the pond. Most of the rest of the plants will not need or even tolerate constant inundation; rather they will live where soil is saturated for all or part of the season (figure 6.16).

Indigenous marsh plants are accustomed to a late summer *drawdown* period when water levels drop and most flower and set seed. It is quite easy to install some plants too deeply at first, and their roots will rot. It is best to design the edge of your pond for maximum flexibility, enabling the roots of your plants to find (if they have not already drowned) the moisture level that best suits them. The simplest way to achieve this is through a wide, gradual slope from level grade a depth of six inches, the maximum depth most marsh plants will tolerate. You may want to leave one section with a wide shelf at the six-inch depth, since there are shrubs such as buttonbush and willows that will thrive there. Your pond edge will look more natural if you vary the width of the edge. It is better to group any shrubs together at one end of the pond so that they do not overwhelm the wildflowers. (At midday, that is where your frogs will be, cooling off in damp soil under the shrubs.) To a certain extent, placement of the grasses and wildflowers will be determined by their moisture requirements, but within those limits, there is plenty of room for creativity.

Swamp

Forested wetlands are some of our loveliest plant communities; probably also our most neglected. Certainly, they cannot be reproduced in all locations. It is not likely that you can contain the water for a swamp in the same way that you can contain a pond, because the roots of the trees would have nowhere to go. Fortunately, most swamp plants tolerate wider ranges of moisture than marsh plants and are far more tolerant of prolonged periods of drought. In fact, swamp trees such as pin oaks, red maple, and green ash are some of our most commonly planted street trees because of their adaptability to a wide range of conditions.

If you have a large stormwater pond, an area with poor drainage, maybe at the bottom of a steep hillside, or where many springs are located, it may be just the spot for a swamp. There are many types to choose from, as many as there are dominant tree species. There are cedar swamps, with northern white cedar common further north and Atlantic white cedar dominating further south. Formerly covering vast areas, these naturally occurring communities are now rare, especially Atlantic cedar. There are hardwood swamps, including communities dominated by silver maple, sweetgum, or swamp white oak (figure 6.17). There are also many kinds of shrub swamps (figure 6.18).

Figure 6.17. This swamp forms the outer edge of a small cranberry bog. The sphagnum mat in the center gives the appearance of a mowed path. Red maples, tupelo, black spruce, serviceberry, wild azaleas, and many different ferns, wildflowers, and sedges are found here.

Figure 6.18. Large clumps of cinnamon ferns give this swamp an almost primeval appearance. Besides the ferns, this shrub swamp is dominated by highbush blueberries, with an occasional hemlock and red maple at the edge.

....

Table 6.10.

Swamp

Trees

Acer rubrum, red maple	*Liquidambar styraciflua*, sweetgum
Acer saccharinum, silver maple	*Nyssa sylvatica*, black gum
Chamaecyparis thyoides, Atlantic white cedar	*Quercus* bicolor, swamp white oak
	Quercus palustris, pin oak
Fraxinus pennsylvanica, green ash	*Thuja occidentalis*, northern white cedar
Larix laricina, larch	*Ulmus americana*, American elm

Shrubs

Aronia melanocarpa, black chokeberry	*Rhododendron viscosum*, swamp honeysuckle
Cephalanthus occidentalis, buttonbush	
Clethra alnifolia, sweet pepperbush	*Rosa palustris*, swamp rose
Ilex verticillata, winterberry	*Sambucus canadensis*, elderberry
Lindera benzoin, spicebush	*Sorbus americana*, mountain ash
Potentilla fruticosa, shrubby cinquefoil	*Viburnum cassinoides*, wild raisin
Rhododendron periclymenoides, pinxter-bloom azalea	

Wildflowers

Arisaema triphyllum, Jack-in-the-pulpit	*Maianthemum canadense*, Canada mayflower
Caltha palustris, marsh marigold	
Cornus canadensis, bunchberry	*Senecio obovatus*, golden ragwort
Impatiens capensis, jewelweed	*Symplocarpus foetidus*, skunk cabbage
Lilium superbum, Turk's cap lily	*Viola cucullata*, marsh blue violet

Grasses and Ferns

Carex stricta, tussock sedge	*Osmunda cinnamomea*, cinnamon fern
Hystrix patula, bottlebrush grass	Osmunda regalis, royal fern

....

Before beginning your design, try to seek out examples close to home and study them throughout the seasons, noting how the plants adapt to different moisture levels. If you are starting from scratch, it will be important to provide extra moisture during droughts for the first few growing seasons, until trees have had a chance to establish extensive root systems. The list of suggested plants includes wildflowers; most will not survive unless the trees have already formed adequate shade.

Bog

Like an upland heath or a salt marsh, bogs have that well-organized natural community look simply because plants grow where they must. Kettle-hole bogs, formed when the glacier left behind immense chunks of ice, sometimes form concentric rings of vegetation, from taller shrubs on the outermost edge, then shorter shrubs, to the center of the bog where a floating mat of mosses is carpeted by the lowest-growing plants—the cranberries, pitcher plants, and sundews. Bog shrubs flower from early spring until the pitcher plants open their showy, long-lasting blooms; in autumn the leaves of many bog plants turn amazing shades of scarlet and plum.

Carnivorous bog plants are becoming quite popular just now, partly because of some excellent work done by American plant breeders using our amazingly diverse pitcher plants. In addition to using their green leaves to photosynthesize for sugars, these fascinating plants also trap insects and digest them for additional nutrients (figure 6.19). Some collectors keep pitcher plants and sundews in terrariums, but a more natural display is

Figure 6.19. This fortunate pitcher plant has captured a meal. If heavy rains come before digestion occurs, the insect may be washed out onto the sphagnum mat.

Table 6.11.

Bogs

Bog Plants

Andromeda glaucophylla, bog rosemary	*Rhododendron canadense*, rhodora
Chamaedaphne calyculata, leatherleaf	*Sarracenia* spp., pitcher plants
Drosera rotundifolia, sundew	*Sphagnum* spp., mosses
Kalmia angustifolia, sheep laurel	*Vaccinium macrocarpon*, cranberry
Ledum groenlandicum, Labrador tea	

preferable. Bogs can be created in much the same way as ponds, with liners or containers. One of the ways in which a created bog differs from a pond is in the use of a much more shallow basin to maintain a consistently moist mixture of sand and organic matter, but without standing water. It is important not to use overly fertile soil or to add fertilizer, which is toxic to bog plants; the soil mix should be lean and acidic. Do not water your bog with chlorinated water.

THE SEASHORE

It never fails to amaze me that plants take so well to sand. I think there must be more plants that thrive in sand than clay. I look at a densely vegetated sand dune in amazement, wondering how the roots of those plants manage to keep the water from just flowing right through the sand and back into the sea. Of course, the water does not flow back to sea but rather sinks to the water table, and that is how far the roots need to go. It is those same roots that keep the sand from washing out to sea. The factor that limits the choice of plants for seaside locations, then, is not the amount of sand, it is the amount of salt. The closer one gardens to the seashore, the fewer plants can tolerate even the salt spray that is deposited on leaves. In situations like this, indigenous plants are truly the gardener's best friends.

Salt Heath, Shrubland, and Grassland

Seaside plant communities are in a relatively constant state of disturbance, owing to the action of wind and waves. Perhaps for this reason, they bear strong

---

Table 6.12.

Salt Heath, Shrubland, and Grassland

Seaside Shrubs and Trees

Amelanchier canadensis, shadbush	*Prunus maritima*, beach plum
Ilex opaca, American holly	*Prunus serotina*, black cherry
Juniperus virginiana, eastern red cedar	*Quercus stellata*, post oak
Myrica pensylvanica, bayberry	*Rhus coppalinum*, shining sumac
Pinus rigida, pitch pine	*Rosa virginiana*, Virginia rose

Low Seaside Shrubs and Vines

Arctostaphylos uva-ursi, bearberry	*Rosa carolina*, Carolina rose
Gaylussacia baccata, black huckleberry	*Rubus flagellaris*, northern dewberry
Hudsonia tomentosa, beach heather	*Vaccinium angustifolius*, lowbush
Lathyrus japonicus, beach pea	blueberry

Seaside Meadow or Grassland

Ammophila breviligulata, beach grass	*Liatris scariosa* var. *novae-angliae*, New
Antennaria plantaginifolia, pussytoes	England blazing star
Aster dumosum, bushy aster	*Limonium carolinianum*, sea lavender
Aster linariifolius, pine-leaved aster	*Panicum virgatum*, panic grass
Danthonia spicata, poverty grass	*Schizachyrium scoparium*, little
Deschampsia flexuosa, common	bluestem
hairgrass	*Solidago sempervirens*, seaside
Euthamia graminifolia, flat-top	goldenrod
goldenrod	*Sorghastrum nutans*, Indian grass

---

resemblances to the inland successional plant communities discussed above and include some of the same plants. Similarly, there are no rigid boundaries between dunes and shrubland, or heath and grassland; all intermingle in a shifting mosaic, as constantly changing site conditions dictate. If you have never seen any of these natural seashore communities in a healthy condition, I strongly urge you to do so before attempting to recreate one. Protected areas in state and national seashores have beautiful examples of untrampled dunes and swales fully carpeted by layers of interlocking shades of green. In fall, the carpet changes from green to shades of wine, plum, and scarlet. This may be the best season to view these increasingly rare plant communities.

The characteristics of your site and your own personal preferences will determine which plant community dominates your seaside mosaic: heath, grassland or shrubland. (Those gardeners who really enjoy tilting at windmills could even attempt to recreate the magnificent maritime holly forest located at Sandy Hook, New Jersey.) All of the plants listed in this section are salt-tolerant and found naturally along the seashore. The list is organized loosely according to communities, in order to facilitate a design that emphasizes one community over another. In all cases, however, gardeners should feel quite free to mix and match; all of these plants can be found growing in close proximity at one site or another.

Salt Marsh

On the other side of the seashore lie the relatively undisturbed plant communities of the estuary. Protected by the barrier beach from the worst of the wind and waves, the salt marshes and high salt meadows are bordered by shrubs at the upland edges. Like heaths, salt meadows always manage to look well-maintained and bring joy to the heart of the compulsively neat gardener. Whenever I have had the rare opportunity to walk in one, I find myself unable to resist stroking the low, softly undulating waves of salt meadow grass as if the entire meadow were a great furry animal (figure 6.20). By law, only trained professionals can work in these regulated areas. If you own a portion of a salt marsh, you must check with your local and/or state environmental agency before beginning a project that would involve disturbing any part of your property that even comes close to a regulated area.

Generally speaking, if a permit is issued to plant in a regulated area, indigenous wetland plants must be used. For this reason, these specialized plants are readily available for purchase. It is a good idea for owners of salt marshes and other wetland plant communities to be familiar with them. Many of these plants would also be perfectly happy in your nearby upland garden and would work to unify your home with the surrounding landscape. Rose-mallow, in particular, is a colorful addition to any garden; numerous cultivars are readily available at local nurseries.

The foregoing plant lists are meant as examples only. Mixing and matching is fine, and, as your own observations will confirm, there is a great deal of overlap as plant communities merge into one another. One of the great pleasures of this type of gardening is the opportunity to take field trips to confirm details and see the wild plants you want to use in their natural habitat. Remember, however, that your garden is still a garden, not a natural area

Figure 6.20. The low marsh has taller grasses and begins in the intertidal zone, where it is subjected to twice-daily tides. The high marsh, with its much lower grasses, sits just above the daily ebb and flow but is completely immersed during especially high tides and storms.

restoration project. Feel free to experiment. The wildlife that need the plants you have put in your garden will find them, whether or not you have created a picture-perfect, textbook example of a natural plant community.

Table 6.13.
Salt Marsh

Trees and Shrubs

Baccharis halimifolia, groundsel tree

Chamaecyparis thyoides, Atlantic white cedar

Iva frutescens, saltmarsh-elder

Juniperus virginiana, eastern red cedar

Rosa carolina, Carolina rose

Flowering Plants

Aster tenuifolius, slender saltmarsh aster

Hibiscus moscheutos, rose mallow

Limonium carolinianum, sea lavender

High Meadow Grasses

Distichlis spicata, spikegrass

Juncus gerardii, black-grass

Spartina patens, salt-meadow grass

Low Meadow Grasses

Spartina alterniflora, cordgrass

Spartina cynosuroides, big cordgrass

7

SHOPPING FOR

INDIGENOUS TREES,

SHRUBS,

AND PERENNIALS

*I need you to write this book so that I can
go plant shopping without you.*

....

MICHELE HERTZ, SCULPTOR, ILLUSTRATOR

It puzzles some of us that indigenous plants form such a small segment of wholesale and retail nursery offerings. A few clues were gathered, however, during research into the history of indigenous plant use for landscaping purposes. Early on, gardeners clearly had no compunctions about digging wild plants for home use, so perhaps nurseries were unable to induce people to pay money for them. Perhaps the nursery owners themselves felt they were not truly serving the public unless they could offer the consumer a product that was not available elsewhere for free. They needed to sell something new, something special, something exotic. Meanwhile, many of these same nurseries were exporting boatloads of indigenous plants to Europe. Clearly, long-term psychological, cultural, and financial dynamics have combined to create today's international nursery industry.

Now, however, the tables have turned. Instead of being surrounded by a healthy, indigenous, wild landscape as our pioneer ancestors were, we are surrounded by woodlots overrun by garden escapes; it is the cultured landscapes that have gone wild. And instead of digging these all-too-common invasive plants from the wild and putting them back in our gardens, knowledgeable gardeners, high school environmental clubs, and conservation-minded volunteers are trying to kill them off or at least control them from reproducing further. Because now we know how truly harmful they are.

Knowing how we got to this point may make it easier to change the existing dynamics that favor the increased production of nonindigenous over indigenous plants. Gardeners have the most important role to play. The nursery industry is reminiscent of the American auto industry, still peddling the same old models instead of the innovative products we need for twenty-first-century living. Indigenous plants will be the sustainable landscape of the future. If enough gardeners refuse to purchase the same species the nursery industry has sold for the past one hundred years (dressed up, of course, in the latest fashion colors and variegated leaves), and resist the temptation to buy their latest newly imported exotic species, the industry will be forced to change. Insist on indigenous. The rest of this chapter will explore the many ways well-informed gardeners can find the plants they need, and at the same time, send a message to their own local nurseries.

FIND TRUSTED SOURCES OF INFORMATION

It is unrealistic to assume that all nursery or landscape professionals will know whether a given species is indigenous or not. Misinformation of all kinds abounds. In discussing Norway maples with a well-informed nursery professional, I was told that his nursery no longer carried Norway maples. When I pointed to a nearby ball-and-burlapped specimen of 'Crimson King' (the purple-leaved Norway maple cultivar), I was informed that the seeds of 'Crimson King' are not viable, so it was fine to offer it for sale. Because no one at the nursery had ever seen a purple Norway maple growing outside of a cultivated landscape, the fatal assumption was made that it was a sterile clone, despite the fact that most cultivars do not come true from seed. In other words, 'Crimson King' could be seeding itself all over the landscape, disguised in green leaves.

For most nurseries, place of origin simply is not considered relevant. That obviously is not true of the many fine specialty nurseries, some of which sell only indigenous species. The average nursery professional, however, will ask about your garden and will correctly prescribe plants that will grow well for your garden's conditions; they think inside the box, not about the larger landscape outside your garden. It is simply not part of basic training.

Once we know where not to go for information, we need to know alternative trusted sources. Fortunately, there is no shortage of excellent reference books, many of which are included in the bibliography. The Internet has revolutionized plant research. There are several excellent online databases specifically for indigenous plants. Finally, there is nothing like talking to a real person. If there is a native plant society near you, staff may be able to answer your questions about plants or help you to find local nurseries or landscape designers that specialize in selling and using indigenous plants. One example, the Native Plant Center at Westchester Community College, the first local affiliate of the national Lady Bird Johnson Wildflower Center, provides educational services to the greater New York metropolitan region. If you already belong to a local garden club, perhaps you and other like-minded gardeners can form a subcommittee devoted to learning more about indigenous plants and sharing the information with the rest of your club.

VISITING NURSERIES

Prior to setting foot inside any nursery, it is useful to analyze your garden's needs and make a list of the plants you want. In the best-case scenario, you will have worked out a design, perhaps even sketched it, so that you have an idea of the quantities of plants needed to fill a given area. Visiting a nursery without a list can be overwhelming to the novice and dangerous to both your pocketbook and the environment. It is likely that all of the scientific names you have carefully memorized will exit your brain as you stare at the colorful displays surrounding you. The temptations discussed earlier, such as the urge to be the first on your block to plant an exotic specimen, will be more difficult to fight, absent a detailed shopping list.

Of course, when you visit a nursery, you will see plants that are not on your shopping list, plants that you never knew existed and that might be indigenous, that you would really like to have. Pick out the most beautiful specimen and ask the nursery staff to hold it for you. Explain that you simply do not have room for it in your car today. Then go home and find out more about the plant. Do not ask the nursery staff to tell you whether or not a plant is indigenous (or even native). I have actually had nursery staff tell me, in complete sincerity, that all of their plants are native, because they were all grown at the nursery. Many of them simply will not understand your question and, to be helpful, will tell you what they think you want to hear.

Once you know the plants you are looking for, it is not difficult to find them. Knowing the scientific names of the plants you want makes it that much more certain that the nursery will provide, and you will actually purchase, the plants you are seeking. All reputable nurseries label their plants with both common and scientific names. It is, in fact, illegal in New York State to sell unlabeled plants. Plants occasionally can be mislabeled. Tags will go missing, in which case it is definitely a "buyer beware" situation. Some plant tags only list the first half, or genus, of the scientific name, leaving the exact species in doubt. It is an annoying, but frequent, practice with cultivars and hybrids. Your recourse is to ask one of the nursery staff to check the records or to go home or to the library and try to research the plant on the Internet or in reference books.

The most common mistake made when purchasing plants—and I am guilty of making it—is using the common name when requesting the plant you want. Early on, when I was redesigning the entrance to our home, I went to a nursery to purchase a pair of arborvitae. The nurseryman showed me a gorgeous pair of mature specimens, the last two. I happily purchased them,

Using the Internet to Determine Origins of Species

Thanks to the Internet, it is now as simple as a few clicks of the mouse to find out whether or not a plant is indigenous to your region. Two useful sites are the U.S. Department of Agriculture's PLANTS database, at http://www.plants.usda.gov, and the Lady Bird Johnson Wildflower Center's database, at http://www.wildflower.org/plants. The Nature Conservancy's database, NatureServe Explorer, at http://www.natureserve.org/explore, is another useful resource. At any of these, simply type the name of the plant you want to learn about into the box labeled "search." You can select either the scientific name or common name option. Many times, I will check more than one site, because the information is complementary. For example, the Wildflower Center database lists the individual states to which a plant is indigenous, whereas the USDA provides maps showing the current range of plants, some of which have naturalized or spread into other states. One word of caution: type carefully; the search engine cannot find your plant if there is the slightest spelling error. You can also simply enter the name of the plant into any commercial search engine, which will offer close substitutes if you make a typo. This is especially useful for hybrids and cultivars, most of which are not covered by any of these sites.

and waited impatiently for delivery. As they were being installed, I glanced at the receipt and almost choked. The scientific name was carefully written down: *Thuja plicata*, in other words, western arborvitae from the Pacific Coast. The species can grow to be a couple of hundred feet high. Fortunately, these were dwarf cultivars. Even so, they are now dwarfing our house.

Sometimes common names can be downright deceiving. When I see the common name American boxwood prominently displayed on a nursery label, it is enough to make me wonder. Boxwood (*Buxus sempervirens*), has always been, and will always be, a plant introduced from Europe. There is no such thing as American boxwood, except in the imagination of the nursery industry. Some of the cultivar names can also be unintentionally deceptive. A shopper might easily think, looking at a plant named *Viburnum ×* 'Chippewa,' that it would be safe to assume one was purchasing an indigenous viburnum. Yet, 'Chippewa' viburnum is a hybrid with two Asian species, *V. japonicum* and *V. dilatatum*, as parents.

Fortunately, quite a few indigenous plants are staples of the trade and can readily be found at almost any nursery, including outlets such as Home Depot and other big box stores. Appendix M provides a list of indigenous plants regularly found at local garden centers. Although commonly available, they are hardly overused, compared with popular nonindigenous plants, and they represent some of the toughest, most reliable and beautiful plants available. Remember that the nursery is not selling them because they are indigenous; they may not even be aware of that fact; they are selling them because those are the plants that have proven themselves and are in demand. One could design a lovely garden, attractive to birds, butterflies, and people, using only these common indigenous plants.

Request Indigenous Plants

If your local nursery does not carry one of the more common plants on your list, in all likelihood it will be able to find it for you. When you place your order, be sure to let the staff know why this particular plant is important to you, including the fact that it is indigenous. At the same time, you might try asking for one of the more hard-to-find plants on your list. In this way, you can expand the nursery's offerings and educate it about your needs.

Make sure your local nursery knows about the American Beauties program (http://www.abnativeplants.com). This is a line of indigenous plants,

Table 7.1.

Caution: These Congeners May Be Easily Confused with One Another

Nonindigenous	Indigenous
Alnus glutinosa, European alder	*Alnus incana* subsp. *rugosa*, speckled alder
Betula platyphylla, Asian white birch	*Betula papyrifera*, paper birch
Carpinus betulus, European hornbeam	*Carpinus caroliniana*, blue beech
Platanus × *hybrida*, London plane tree	*Platanus occidentalis*, sycamore
Viburnum opulus var. *opulus*, guelder rose	*Viburnum opulus* var. *americanum* (*trilobum*), cranberrybush

many common and some not-so-common, marketed and sold to local nurseries throughout the Northeast by a partnership between two enlightened wholesale nurseries, North Creek in Pennsylvania and Pride's Corner Farm in Connecticut. For every American Beauties plant purchased, the partnership makes a donation to the National Wildlife Federation, providing a double benefit for wildlife when you buy it. The American Beauties program is planning to expand to other areas with regionally appropriate plants. If your local nursery is not carrying plants from this program, be sure to ask for them.

Nonindigenous Imposters

Some plants are routinely mislabeled. For example, European guelder rose is often sold as American highbush cranberry. As discussed in chapters 4 and 5, a few of the congeners are quite similar in look and habit. In fact, a very few are so alike that the only differences are minor botanical details. In other words, unless you are an insect or a botanist, you probably will have a difficult time telling these species apart, and the same goes for most nursery workers. Some common plants that could easily be confused are listed in table 7.1. If you are interested in obtaining one of them, and you do not have a trusted native plant nursery to purchase from, it is a good idea to familiarize yourself with the details of their identification and carefully examine the plant before you buy it.

Specialty Nurseries

For computer-savvy gardeners, the Internet has made it very simple to locate almost any plant. It is still true, however, that many indigenous plants are not widely known and propagated, including some of the plants I recommend in this book. For those plants, a trip to your nearest specialty nursery (the one specializing in indigenous plants) is your best bet. Some native plant societies, such as the Native Plant Center at Westchester Community College, have annual sales (figure 7.1). If you do not live near any native plant nursery or native plant society, mail order is a definite option. There are a great many excellent native plant nurseries that conduct a large percentage of their business through mail order. Personally, with rare exceptions, I have had excellent results with plants that I have received through the mail.

If you do have a local native plant nursery, you are in luck (figure 7.2). There is no better source of information. Some offer in-house design services. Most of the smaller, independent native plant growers and retailers (which most of them are) use pesticides only in a true emergency and most of their standard practices would be considered organic. They have inter-

Figure 7.1. Many native plant societies have annual sales, such as this one held by the Native Plant Center on the campus of Westchester Community College.

Figure 7.2. This native plant nursery, Catskill Native Nursery, hosts an annual wild-flower festival.

esting and unusual plants, a fact noted by one of my relatives on a recent trip to the local native plant nursery. She remarked that it was different and so much more interesting than the regular garden centers that all carried the same plants. Perhaps we are coming full circle, and the exotics will be seen as common, and the indigenous will seem exotic. A list of native plant and other selected specialty nurseries, some of which accept mail orders, is found in appendix L.

Other types of specialty nurseries may be unexpected but rewarding places to find unusual indigenous plants, often cultivars that are not in mass production. Those that specialize in conifers are a good example, where one can often find more than a dozen cultivars of arborvitae and white pine. Because the goal of the specialty nursery is to cater to the plant collector, species are offered from every corner of the globe, rather like a botanical garden. Happily, North America is usually well-represented. Some sellers specialize in groups of plants such as woodland plants or rock garden plants (alpines), whereas others concentrate on a particular genus or family, *Rhododendron* being a common example. By the way, the wildlife you wish to attract to your garden will not care whether your plants are dwarf, weeping, or otherwise contorted, so let your imagination run wild.

Nursery-Propagated versus Wild-Collected

It is important, especially when purchasing some of the more unusual indigenous plants, to understand the terminology used to distinguish sustainable propagation methods from unsustainable collecting methods. The best way to be sure that your plant was not collected from the wild is to buy *nursery-propagated* plants from a reliable, trusted nursery source. You will pay more, but your conscience will be clear. Nursery-propagated means that the plant was propagated from seed or cuttings by a nursery that owns, controls, or otherwise has access to the parent plants. The term *nursery-grown* means that small plants were obtained, either from a wholesaler that sells baby plants (*plugs* or *liners*) or, possibly, collected from the wild, and grown on, usually to blooming size, in the nursery. Because of the difficulty in determining, at the point of purchase, whether liners or wild-collected material were used, these plants are best avoided unless you know and trust the grower.

The term *wild-collected* seems self-explanatory, but there are different permutations. Wild collecting can refer to digging up the entire plant, or taking only parts of the plant, including seeds. At the present time, given the pressures our native plant communities face, the only permissible reason to remove entire plants from the wild is if they face certain destruction from the bulldozer or chainsaw sitting next to them. Actually, plants taken in this way are not considered wild-collected; the practice is considered *plant salvage*, but it should only be undertaken in the company of a person trained in indigenous plant horticulture. There is no way, unfortunately, to know at the point of purchase whether or not your wild-collected plant was rescued or simply dug for profit. Anyone who is selling wild-collected plants would

....

Nursery-propagated: Plants that are propagated from seeds or cuttings of parent stock owned or controlled either by the nursery itself or by its trusted sources, either commercial or nonprofit.

Nursery-grown: Small plants were obtained, either from another commercial source that propagated them from seeds or cuttings or else from wild-collected stock, and grown to larger size for sale by a nursery.

Wild-collected: Plant materials, including seeds, roots, cuttings, or entire plants, that were taken from natural areas for sale.

....

Figure 7.3. Advances in horticultural practices have made it possible to offer plants, such as these red trilliums (*Trillium erectum*), that have been propagated by specialty nurseries. There is no longer any need to collect these plants from the wild.

like you to believe that the plant was rescued, whether or not it was. Mail order nurseries that sell woodland plants for a few dollars each are almost certainly selling wild-collected plants. A common sense rule of thumb to follow when purchasing plants concerns price: if it seems too good to be true, then it probably is.

Some nurseries own their own woodlands and collect their own plants for sale. Given that some of them have been in operation for quite a few years, presumably, they are managing to produce plants on a reasonably sustainable basis. Whether or not such plants would be considered nursery-propagated or wild-collected is an interesting question. A more proactive nursery industry might promulgate standards and consistent terminology for the propagation and sale of indigenous plants to assist unwary customers.

There is no longer any need to purchase wild-collected plants. Horticulturists specializing in propagating indigenous plants have cracked the code on some, such as trilliums and certain orchids, formerly considered almost impossible to propagate from seed (figure 7.3). Tissue culture, which has revolutionized nursery propagation in general, has also done wonders for indigenous plant culture, greatly reducing the amount of time it takes baby plants to grow to blooming size.

DECIDING HOW MANY PLANTS TO BUY

One can spend a great deal of time determining exactly how many plants will fit into a given space, and for large, complex jobs, it is an important task. If you are planning your garden from scratch, it is a good idea to do this. If you have hired a landscaper, he or she will do this for you. If you prefer to pick out your own plants, you can have the landscaper give you the total quantities needed for each plant. The one caveat to this approach is whether the person calculating totals does so according to size of plant at maturity, by far the most common, straightforward method. This is a fine approach in many situations. If, however, the plants you have chosen are slow growing, and you are planting very young plants, you can be left looking at a sea of wood chips dotted with islands of plants, plus extra maintenance in keeping the wood chips free of invading weeds, for quite a while.

The simplest solution is more plants and tighter spacing. The garden will look better sooner and, strangely enough, plants like the company of other plants. It will add to the up-front costs, but you should save on maintenance. At some point, you may have to thin out a few stragglers that become overwhelmed by the competition, but this is a small price to pay for the instant garden look. The concept of succession, discussed in the previous chapter, also can be useful in this situation. Knowing in advance that some plants will take time to grow in, you can put some fast-growing, short-lived plants between them, with the understanding that at some future point they will be shaded out or otherwise competitively excluded.

As you can see, determining the number of plants by mathematical formula will produce a certain look, but not necessarily the one you want. Your overall design goals should influence the type and manner of plant spacing. You may want the opposite of a lush, dense planting; perhaps more of a minimalist approach, where every individual plant is seen to best effect.

By far the more common dilemma for the plant buyer is how many new plants to add to an existing garden. This is where higher math and I depart company, except that I obey the rule of three. Unless the plant in question is an expensive experiment or a specimen tree, always buy at least three or five, or in multiples of three or five. Just as there are no straight lines, there are no even numbers in the natural landscape. There are exceptions for formal landscapes; one never buys just two plants, but rather a consciously matched pair for a specific purpose, to frame an entry, for example. But generally speaking, odd-numbered groupings always seem to fit better into the garden.

FRUITING PLANTS

Another variable comes into play when purchasing fruiting plants. Particularly if you have chosen any dioecious plants (see chapter 3 and appendix D for an explanation and plant list), you will need to plant two or more. Plants with which the nursery industry has a long history, such as hollies and junipers, will usually be labeled as male or female. Do not be confused, however, by cultivar names; the holly 'Dan Fenton' is a female. For species that have little history of cultivation, however, such as spicebush, you might as well flip a coin. If coin flipping goes well, you will get one male and one female plus berries. If you are purchasing small plants at a good price, consider buying three or five and eventually replacing any extra males. If the plant is old enough to flower, there is the scientific method. Study the flower forms and visit the nursery when the plants are in bloom; pick out the best-looking male and a few female companions. You may be there awhile; the nursery staff will probably co-opt you into helping other customers.

Single specimens of cherries (*Prunus* spp.), juneberries (*Amelanchier* spp.), and other monoecious plants will fruit, but sparsely, unless your neighbors also have them, as there will be no opportunity for cross-pollination. If you have the room, planting fruiting plants in masses will produce the best results for both monoecious and dioecious plants and your feathered friends.

Having set forth some of the pitfalls of plant shopping and how to avoid them, I hope you find your shopping expeditions as interesting and full of pleasant surprises as I do. It is always exciting to find an indigenous plant where I least expect to, say, at Wal-Mart or Home Depot, for example. Even when I am not buying any plants, it is always fun and educational to look. Some of us window shop on Fifth Avenue and some of us would rather window shop at any and every nursery; diversity makes the world go round.

AFTERWORD

Within our children's lifetimes it is possible, in some regions inevitable, that all land will be spoken for, either built on or set aside as preserved land. So-called vacant land, with the exception of strip-mining and Superfund sites, will be gone. For those of us who see this trend as decadence, rather than progress, it can be difficult to avoid the temptation to pour sugar in the fuel tank of every bulldozer one sees.

For better or worse, humans are a force of nature, as surely as the glaciers that rearranged landscapes and biological systems thousands of years ago. In impact, however, we are closer to an earthquake or volcano because of the speed with which we are changing the world. The glaciers gave plants and animals time to adjust to drastic climate change, whereas in barely two centuries, humanity's Industrial Revolution has managed to fast-forward planetary warming at an unprecedented rate. As responsible members of the human race, we need to take actions that will slow the runaway train; we need to give ourselves and the other species with which we share this planet time to adjust to inevitable change.

For thousands of years, in the wake of the glaciers and prior to European contact, humans managed this continent with a light hand and thrived on the bounty of a rich and productive landscape. These peoples were part and parcel of the natural world. They embodied what we call sustainability. Peering backward into prehistory, we can regain our optimism. We are part of the natural world around us, and we can be a positive force as well as a negative one. If, however, we see ourselves as apart from nature, or above nature, we will fail to act or fail to act responsibly. If we remove top predators from ecosystems and either do not take their place or fail to reintroduce top predators, forested landscapes will crash. If we strip-mine indigenous vegetation, dump it on the compost pile, and replace it with nonindigenous vegetation that supports nothing but our overdeveloped sense of aesthetics, bird and butterfly populations will crash. If we do not control the biological pollution we have unleashed, even our carefully preserved landscapes will disappear under a mass of twisted vines.

The choice is ours. As gardeners, we are fortunately endowed with love for a hobby that has profound potential for positive change. By making the switch from nonindigenous to indigenous plants we can literally reconnect the landscape with its inhabitants. It is my hope that this book has shown that it can be a relatively painless transition—that we simply do not need plants from around the world when there is such a rich variety of indigenous flora to choose from. As we expand our gardening habits to include stewardship of our surrounding natural areas through the thoughtful planting of indigenous plants in our own gardens, we may bask in the knowledge that it is possible to have loads of fun at the same time we are making a better world.

APPENDIXES

A. CIRCUMBOREAL PLANTS

Below is a partial listing of plants that were able to migrate widely during interglacial periods, forming an interesting class of vegetation known as circumpolar or circumboreal flora. These plants are indigenous to more than one region, even in some cases, to more than one continent.

Achillea millefolium, yarrow
Arctostaphylos uva-ursi, bearberry
Athyrium filix-femina, lady fern
Calla palustris, wild calla lily
Caltha palustris, marsh marigold
Campanula rotundifolia, bluebells of Scotland
Drosera rotundifolia, round-leaf sundew
Epilobium (Chamerion) angustifolium, fireweed
Hierochloe odorata, sweet grass
Juniperus communis, common juniper
Linnaea borealis, twinflower
Mentha arvensis, field mint
Oenothera biennis, common evening primrose
Osmunda regalis, royal fern
Potentilla (Dasiphora) fruticosa, shrubby cinquefoil
Potentilla norvegica, rough cinquefoil
Prunella vulgaris subsp. *lanceolata*, self-heal
Pteridium aquilinum, bracken fern
Rosa acicularis, prickly rose
Rubus idaeus subsp. *strigosus*, red raspberry
Sambucus racemosa (pubens), red elder
Typha latifolia, cattail
Vaccinium vitis-idaea subsp. *minus*, lingonberry

B. NECTAR PLANTS THAT SERVE AS HOSTS

Below is a suggested list of plants that not only attract adult butterflies and moths with nectar but also serve as hosts for their caterpillars. A continual floral display will attract the greatest diversity of species; for this reason, season of bloom is given for each plant listed.

Species	Season of Bloom
Arabis spp., rock cresses	spring
Asclepias spp., milkweeds	summer
Aster spp., asters	fall
Ceanothus americanus, New Jersey tea	summer
Epilobium spp., willow-herbs	summer
Eupatorium (*Eupatoriadelphus*) spp., Joe-Pye weeds	summer–fall
Eupatorium perfoliatum, boneset	summer
Euthamia graminifolia, grass-leaved goldenrod	late summer
Fragaria virginiana, strawberry	spring
Geranium maculatum, wild geranium	spring
Helenium autumnale, Helen's flower	late summer
Helianthemum canadense, frostweed	fall
Helianthus decapetalus, woodland sunflower	summer
Heliopsis helianthoides, oxeye daisy	summer
Hibiscus moscheutos, rose mallow	summer–fall
Hypericum spp., St. John's worts	summer
Iris versicolor, blue flag iris	early summer
Liatris spp., blazing stars	late summer
Monarda spp., beebalms	summer
Oenothera spp., evening primroses	summer
Phlox spp., phlox	spring–summer
Rudbeckia spp., black-eyed Susans	summer–fall
Sanguinaria canadensis, bloodroot	earliest spring
Senecio (*Packera*) *aurea*, golden ragwort	spring
Solidago spp., goldenrods	summer–fall
Verbena hastata, blue vervain	summer
Vernonia spp., ironweeds	summer–fall
Veronicastrum virginicum, Culver's root	summer
Viola spp., violets (avoid nonindigenous *Viola odorata* and *V. tricolor*)	spring
Zizia aurea, golden Alexanders	spring

C. BERRIES FOR BIRDS

These hardy shrubs and trees will thrive in a wide range of soils and will fruit best in full sun. All will fruit even better with cross-pollination, so plant more than one of each species. Three species are dioecious, as indicated; they will require at least one male and one female to produce fruit. Once established, all are tough and drought-tolerant. Fruiting season is indicated for all plants; some have berries that ripen in fall but hang on throughout the winter, providing food for residents, as well as early spring migrants. Planting a mix of many different species as a hedge or border will attract birds all year long.

Fruiting Shrubs	Fruiting Season
Amelanchier canadensis, shadbush ('Glennform' is particularly good for hedges)	early summer
Aronia (*Photinia*) *arbutifolia*, red chokeberry	winter
Aronia (*Photinia*) *melanocarpa*, black chokeberry	winter
Cornus alternifolia, pagoda dogwood	late summer
Cornus amomum, silky dogwood	summer
Cornus racemosa, gray dogwood	late summer
Cornus sericea, red-twig dogwood	fall
Corylus americana, American hazelnut	fall
Crateagus spp. (avoid nonindigenous *monogyna*), hawthorns	winter
Ilex verticillata (need male and female), winterberry	winter
Juniperus virginiana (need male and female), eastern red cedar (also provides shelter in winter)	winter
Myrica (*Morella*) *pensylvanica* (need male and female), bayberry	winter
Prunus pensylvanica, pin cherry	summer
Prunus virginiana, chokecherry	late summer–fall
Rubus spp., raspberries	summer
Sambucus canadensis, elderberry	late summer
Sambucus racemosa (*pubens*), red elder	early summer
Vaccinium corymbosum, highbush blueberry	summer
Vaccinium stamineum, deerberry	fall
Viburnum cassinoides, wild raisin	fall
Viburnum dentatum, arrowwood	late summer
Viburnum lentago, nannyberry	fall
Viburnum nudum, smooth viburnum	fall
Viburnum opulus var. *americanum*, highbush cranberry	winter
Viburnum prunifolium, plum-leaved viburnum	late summer

D. DIOECIOUS PLANTS

This appendix lists many indigenous examples of dioecious species. Unlike most plants, which produce both male and female flowers or flower parts together on the same plant, those listed below have separate male and female plants; at least one of each sex is required for reproduction. Interestingly, some members of the maple (*Acer*) family, though usually dioecious, are capable of producing individual plants that combine both sexes.

Trees

Acer negundo, box elder
Cercis canadensis, redbud
Chionanthus virginicus, fringe tree
Cotinus obovatus, American smoke tree
Diospyros virginiana, persimmon
Fraxinus spp., ashes
Gleditsia triacanthos, honey locust
Gymnocladus dioicus, Kentucky coffee tree
Ilex opaca, American holly
Juniperus virginiana, red cedar
Morus rubra, red mulberry
Nyssa sylvatica, tupelo
Populus spp., aspens
Robinia pseudoacacia, black locust
Salix spp., willows
Sassafras albidum, sassafras
Zanthoxylem americanum, prickly ash

Shrubs

Baccharis halimifolia, sea myrtle
Comptonia peregrina, sweet fern
Ilex, spp., inkberries, winterberries
Juniperus spp., creeping junipers
Lindera benzoin, spicebush

Shrubs, cont.

Myrica pensylvanica, bayberry
Paxistima canbyi, Canby's mountain-lover
Rhus spp., sumacs
Taxus canadensis, Canada yew

Vines

Celastrus scandens, American bittersweet
Clematis verticillaris, rock clematis
Clematis virginiana, virgin's bower
Cocculus carolinus, Carolina snailseed
Menispermum canadense, moonseed
Smilax spp., catbriers
Toxicodendron radicans, poison ivy
Vitis spp., wild grapes

Perennials

Antennaria dioica, pussytoes
Aruncus dioicus, goatsbeard
Epigaea repens, trailing arbutus
Napaea dioica, glade mallow
Thalictrum dioicum, early meadow rue
Thalictrum pubescens, tall meadow rue

E. INVASIVE NONINDIGENOUS PLANTS TO AVOID

The plants listed below (and described in chapter 4) are still offered for sale by nurseries, despite the fact that several have been listed by many states as invasive or noxious. Some states have prohibited the sale of certain species; those states are indicated in parentheses following the plant name. Some plants that have not yet been formally listed already show signs of invasiveness and may appear on updated lists in the future.

Trees

Acer platanoides, Norway maple (Mass.)

Acer pseudoplatanus, sycamore maple

Cornus kousa, Kousa dogwood

Pyrus calleryana (all cvs.), Callery (Bradford) pear

Salix babylonica, weeping willow

Shrubs

Berberis thunbergii, Japanese barberry (Mass.)

Buddleia davidii, butterfly bush

Euonymus alatus, burning bush (Mass.)

Forsythia ×intermedia, showy forsythia

Hibiscus syriacus, rose of Sharon

Lonicera mackii (including 'Rem Red' and other cvs.), Amur honeysuckle (Conn., Mass.)

Lonicera morrowii, Morrow's honeysuckle (Conn., Mass., N.H.)

Lonicera tatarica, Tatarian honeysuckle (Conn., Mass., N.H.)

Lonicera xylosteum, dwarf honeysuckle (Conn.)

Lonicera ×bella, Bell's honeysuckle (Conn., Mass., N.H.)

Salix purpurea, purple-osier willow

Viburnum dilatatum, linden viburnum

Viburnum lantana, wayfaring tree

Viburnum opulus var. *opulus*, guelder rose

Viburnum plicatum, Japanese snowball

Viburnum rhytidophyllum, leatherleaf viburnum

Viburnum setigerum, tea viburnum

Viburnum sieboldii, Siebold's viburnum

Vitex agnus-castus, chaste tree

Vines

Ampelopsis brevipedunculata, porcelain berry (Mass.)
Celastrus orbiculatus, Oriental bittersweet (Conn., Mass., N.H.)
Lonicera japonica, Japanese honeysuckle (Conn., Mass., N.H.)
Wisteria japonica, Japanese wisteria
Wisteria sinensis, Chinese wisteria

Perennials, Grasses, and Groundcovers

Aegopodium podagraria, goutweed (Conn., Mass.)
Cortaderia selloana, pampas grass
Iris pseudacorus, yellow water iris (Conn., Mass., N.H.)
Lythrum salicaria, purple loosestrife (Conn., Mass.)
Miscanthus sinensis, plume grass
Pennisetum spp., fountain grasses (four species banned in Mass.)
Vinca minor, periwinkle

F. INDIGENOUS HEIRLOOMS

The indigenous plants listed below have a long history of landscaping service, as evidenced by the early date of use (in parentheses) documented for some. Not surprisingly, most of these plants are still sold by many nurseries.

Conifers
Abies balsamea, balsam fir (1771)
Juniperus communis 'Hibernica,' common juniper (1872)
Juniperus virginiana, eastern red cedar (1735)
Picea mariana, black spruce (1771)
Pinus strobus, white pine (1771)
Taxodium distichum, bald cypress (1737)
Thuja occidentalis, arborvitae (1783)
Tsuga canadensis, hemlock (1771)

Shade Trees
Acer rubrum, red maple (1771)
Acer saccharinum, silver maple
Acer saccharum, sugar maple (1771)
Catalpa speciosa, northern catalpa
Diospyros virginiana, persimmon (1783)
Fraxinus americana, American ash
Gleditsia triacanthos, honey locust
Juglans nigra, black walnut
Liquidambar styraciflua, sweetgum
Liriodendron tulipifera, tulip tree (1737)
Platanus occidentalis, sycamore
Populus deltoides, cottonwood
Quercus alba, white oak
Quercus palustris, pin oak (1771)
Quercus rubra, red oak
Robinia pseudoacacia, black locust
Sorbus americana, mountain ash
Ulmus americana, American elm

Ornamental Trees

Acer negundo, box elder
Asimina triloba, pawpaw (1783)
Betula lenta, sweet birch (1771)
Betula populifolia, gray birch
Cercis canadensis, redbud (1739)
Cornus florida, flowering dogwood (1735)
Crateagus crus-galli, cockspur hawthorn (1734)
Halesia carolina, Carolina silverbell
Ilex opaca, American holly (1783)
Magnolia acuminata, cucumber magnolia (1736)
Malus ioensis 'Plena,' double-flowered prairie crab apple
Sassafras albidum, sassafras (1771)

Shrubs

Aralia spinosa, devil's walking stick (1783)
Calycanthus floridus, Carolina allspice
Chionanthus virginicus, fringe tree (1735)
Clethra alnifolia, sweet pepperbush
Cornus stolonifera, red-twig dogwood
Corylus americana, American hazelnut (1771)
Euonymus americanus, American strawberrybush (1771)
Hamamelis virginiana, witch hazel
Hydrangea arborescens, snowball hydrangea
Hypericum kalmianum, golden St. John's wort (1787)
Ilex verticillata, winterberry
Kalmia latifolia, mountain laurel (1734)
Lindera benzoin, spicebush (1771)
Magnolia virginiana, sweetbay magnolia (1736)
Myrica pensylvanica, bayberry (1771)
Physocarpus opulifolia, common ninebark
Rhododendron calendulaceum, flame azalea
Rhododendron catawbiense, Catawba rhododendron
Rhododendron maximum, great laurel
Rhododendron viscosum, swamp honeysuckle
Symphoricarpos orbiculatus, coralberry

Vines

Apios americana, groundnut
Aristolochia macrophylla, Dutchman's pipe
Campsis radicans, trumpet creeper
Celastrus scandens, American bittersweet
Clematis virginiana, virgin's bower
Gelsemium sempervirens, Carolina jessamine
Lonicera flava, yellow honeysuckle
Lonicera sempervirens, everlasting honeysuckle
Parthenocissus quinquefolia, Virginia creeper
Wisteria frutescens, American wisteria

Perennials

Aquilegia canadensis, rock bells
Asclepias incarnata, red milkweed
Asclepias tuberosa, butterflyweed
Aster novae-angliae, New England aster (1737)
Baptisia australis, blue wild indigo (1783)
Baptisia tinctoria, yellow wild indigo (1783)
Chasmanthium latifolium, sea oats (grass)
Chelone glabra, turtlehead (1783)
Coreopsis lanceolata, lance-leaf coreopsis
Coreopsis verticillata, whorled tickseed
Delphinium exaltatum, wild larkspur
Echinacea purpurea, purple coneflower
Helenium autumnale, Helen's flower
Hibiscus moscheutos, marsh mallow
Liatris scariosa, blazing star
Liatris spicata, dense blazing star
Lilium canadense, Canada lily
Lilium superbum, superb lily (1738)
Lobelia syphilitica, blue lobelia
Monarda didyma, beebalm
Monarda fistulosum, wild bergamot
Oenothera macrocarpa, Missouri evening primrose
Phlox carolina, Carolina phlox
Phlox maculata, wild sweet William
Phlox paniculata, garden phlox (1737)

Perennials, cont.
Physostegia virginiana, obedient plant
Rudbeckia fulgida, black-eyed Susan
Rudbeckia laciniata, cutleaf coneflower
Tradescantia virginiana, spiderwort
Veronicastrum virginicum, Culver's root
Yucca filamentosa, Adam's needle (1735)

Within Shade Gardens
Anemonella thalictroides, rue anemone
Asarum canadensis, wild ginger (1804)
Dodecatheon meadia, shooting star
Epigaea repens, trailing arbutus
Erythronium americanum, trout lily
Geranium maculatum, wild geranium
Hepatica americana, liverleaf
Mertensia virginica, Virginia bluebells
Mitchella repens, partridgeberry
Mitella diphylla, bishop's cap
Phlox divaricata, woodland phlox
Phlox stolonifera, creeping phlox
Podophyllum peltatum, mayapple
Sanguinaria canadensis, bloodroot
Spigelia marilandica, Indian pink (1783)
Tiarella cordifolia, foamflower
Trillium cernuum, nodding trillium
Trillium erectum, red trillium
Trillium grandiflorum, white trillium
Viola canadensis, Canada violet
Viola pubescens, yellow violet

Within Sunny Rock Gardens
Campanula rotundifolia, harebell
Gaultheria procumbens, wintergreen
Houstonia caerulea, bluet
Phlox subulata, moss phlox (1745)
Viola pedata, bird's-foot violet

Within Water Gardens

Acorus americanus, sweet flag
Caltha palustris, marsh marigold
Gentiana andrewsii, bottle gentian
Iris versicolor, blue flag iris
Lobelia cardinalis, cardinal flower
Mimulus ringens, monkeyflower
Nuphar advena, yellow water lily
Nymphaea odorata, sweet water lily
Orontium aquaticum, golden club
Parnassia caroliniana, grass of Parnassus
Pontederia cordata, pickerelweed
Sagittaria latifolia, duck potato
Veratrum viride, false hellebore (1804)

G. INDIGENOUS PLANTS SUITED FOR JAPANESE AND CHINESE DESIGNS

Listed below are some additional suggestions for alternative indigenous plants to replace some of the more common Japanese and Chinese plants. Many will actually require less intensive maintenance to hold their shape than their Asian counterparts.

Asian Indigenous

Cercis chinensis, Chinese redbud — *Cercis canadensis*, redbud

Chionanthus retusus, Chinese fringe tree — *Chionanthus virginicus*, fringe tree

Hamamelis japonica, Japanese witch hazel — *Hamamelis virginiana*, witch hazel

Ilex crenata, Japanese holly — *Ilex glabra*, inkberry

Ostrya japonica, Japanese hop hornbeam — *Ostrya virginica*, hop hornbeam

Wisteria floribunda, Japanese wisteria — *Wisteria frutescens*, American wisteria

Alternatives for *Acer palmatum*, Japanese Maple

Liquidambar styraciflua 'Gumball,' dwarf sweetgum
Rhus glabra 'Laciniata,' lace-leaved smooth sumac
Sambucus canadensis 'Laciniata,' lace-leaved elderberry
Sambucus racemosa 'Sutherland Gold,' lace-leaved golden elderberry

Alternatives for Japanese Stewartia, *Stewartia pseudocamellia*

Acer pensylvanicum, moosewood
Amelanchier laevis, juneberry
Franklinia alatamaha, Franklin tree
Stewartia ovata, mountain stewartia

Alternatives for Willows, Cherries, and Other Asian Weeping Forms

Cercis canadensis 'Covey,' weeping redbud
Chamaecyparis thyoides 'Glauca Pendula,' weeping Atlantic cedar
Chionanthus virginicus, fringe tree

Alternatives for Willows, Cherries, and Other Asian Weeping Forms, cont.
Juniperus communis 'Oblanga Pendula,' common juniper
Salix amygdaloides, peachleaf willow
Tsuga canadensis 'Cole's Prostrate' and Sargent's Weeping,' weeping
  hemlock

Dwarf, Asymmetrical Conifers
Pinus banksiana 'Schoodic' and 'Uncle Fogy,' jack pine
Pinus strobus 'Contorta,' 'Ottawa,' and 'Shaggy Dog,' white pine

Mounded, Dwarf Conifers to Substitute for Mugo Pine, *Pinus mugo*
Abies balsamea 'Nana,' dwarf balsam fir
Juniperus communis 'Berkshire,' common juniper
Picea mariana 'Ericoides,' black spruce
Pinus strobus 'Paul Waxman' and 'Soft Touch,' white pine
Thuja occidentalis 'Teddy' and 'Danica,' arborvitae

Deciduous Shrubs with Horizontal, Asymmetrical Branching Patterns
Cornus alternifolia, pagoda dogwood
Hamamelis virginiana, witch hazel
Ilex montana, mountain holly
Viburnum lantanoides, hobblebush

Alternatives for Japanese Barberry, *Berberis thunbergii*
Hypericum kalmianum, Kalm's golden St. John's wort
Potentilla fruticosa, shrubby potentilla
Vaccinium angustifolium, lowbush blueberry

H. INDIGENOUS PLANTS
SUITED FOR FORMAL GARDENS

Listed below are some additional suggestions for indigenous plants suitable for use in formal or modernistic landscapes. Their branching patterns form naturally regular shapes that require little pruning to maintain.

Columnar Conifers

Juniperus communis, common juniper
    'Arnold' (to 10 feet, light green)
    'Gold Cone' (slow-growing, gold-tipped)
    'Hibernica' (to 25 feet, deep green)
    'Sentinel' (to 5 feet, blue-green)
Juniperus virginiana, eastern red cedar
    'Glauca' (to 25 feet, blue-tinted)
    'Hillspire' (to 20 feet, deep green)
Picea mariana, black spruce
    'Fastigiata' (slow-growing, deep green, columnar, fastigiate, more open-branched than cedars)
Thuja occidentalis, arborvitae
    'DeGroot's Spire' (under 10 feet, deep green twisted foliage, bronze tint in winter)
    'Malonyana' (full-size to 60 feet, deep green)
    'Smaragd' (under 10 feet, emerald green)
    'Yellow Ribbon' (to 10 feet, bright gold highlights)

Columnar Deciduous Trees

Acer saccharum, sugar maple (slender cultivars may reach full height at maturity)
    'Goldspire'
    'Newton Sentry'
    'Sugar Cone'
    'Temple's Upright'
Amelanchier canadensis, shadbush
    'Glennform' (shrub, 15–20 feet)
Fraxinus pensylvanicus, green ash
    'Cimmaron' (full-height tree)
Liquidambar styraciflua, sweetgum
    'Slender Silhouette' (full-height tree, minimal seedballs)

Spherical Plants

Ilex glabra, inkberry (4–6 feet, depending on cv.)

Thuja occidentalis, arborvitae
    'Danica' (12–18 inches, deep green)
    'Golden Globe' (to 4 feet, with golden highlights)
    'Woodwardii' (4–5 feet, medium green)

I. STREET TREES

The collections of street trees that make up the urban and suburban forests of the Northeast are in need of renewal and diversification. With a few exceptions, the indigenous trees listed below have not been planted extensively. They have all exhibited moderate to high levels of salt tolerance, an important criteria for use along northeastern streets. For those that may be sensitive to soil compaction, tree grates are recommended.

Large Trees (greater than 75 feet at maturity)

Celtis occidentalis, hackberry
Fraxinus americana, American ash . . . . plant seedless male cvs.
Gymnocladus dioicus, Kentucky coffee tree . . . . plant seedless males
Liquidambar styraciflua, sweetgum. . . . . plant fruitless cvs.
Quercus bicolor, swamp white oak
Quercus rubra, red oak . . . . tree grates recommended
Quercus shumardii, Shumard oak
Ulmus americana, American elm . . . . plant disease-resistant cvs.

Medium Trees (50–75 feet at maturity)

Betula lenta, sweet birch . . . . tree grates recommended
Betula nigra, river birch
Betula populifolia, paperbark birch . . . . requires good drainage
Diospyros virginiana, persimmon . . . . males bear no fruit
Fraxinus nigra, black ash. . . . . plant seedless males
Fraxinus pennsylvanica, green ash . . . . plant seedless male cvs.
Gleditsia triacanthos, thornless honey locust . . look for thornless male cvs.
Larix laricina, American larch . . . . deciduous conifer
Nyssa sylvatica, tupelo
Prunus serotina, black cherry
Quercus palustris, pin oak

Small Trees (under 50 feet at maturity)

Crateagus viridis 'Winter King,'
    green hawthorn* . . . . 35 feet, max., bears small thorns
Morus rubra, red mulberry . . . . males bear no fruit
Ostrya virginiana, hop hornbeam. . . . . tree grates recommended
Oxydendron arborea, sourwood . . . . tree grates recommended

Small Trees (under 50 feet at maturity), cont.
Prunus pensylvanicus, pin cherry . . . . tree grates recommended
Prunus virginiana, chokecherry
Prunus virginiana 'Schubert's Red,' purple-leaf chokecherry
Ptelea trifoliata, common hoptree . . . . 35 feet, max.
Quercus imbricaria, shingle oak
Sorbus decora, showy mountain ash* . . . . 35 feet, max.

Salt-Resistant Conifers for Highway Medians and Other Special Situations
Chamaecyparis thyoides, Atlantic white cedar
Juniperus virginiana, eastern red cedar
Thuja occidentalis, arborvitae

*Green hawthorn and showy mountain ash produce bright red clusters of berries that remain on the trees until late winter, or until birds come for them.

J. FRAGRANT AND AROMATIC PLANTS

The indigenous plants listed below all produce either fragrant blossoms or aromatic leaves, twigs, berries, and other plant parts. Although effort was made to include as many plants as possible, this is not an exhaustive list. The intensity of the fragrant or aromatic qualities varies considerably according to the weather, time of day, whether or not the plant has been pollinated, the plant's health and heredity, and the individual plant itself.

Trees

Abies balsamea, balsam fir (aromatic)
Asimina triloba, pawpaw
Betula allegheniensis, yellow birch (aromatic)
Betula lenta, black birch (aromatic)
Castanea dentata, American chestnut
Chionanthus virginicus, fringe tree
Franklinia alatamaha, Franklin tree
Juniperus virginiana, eastern red cedar (aromatic)
Magnolia acuminata, cucumber magnolia
Magnolia virginiana, sweetbay
Malus ioensis, prairie crab apple
Oxydendron arboreum, sourwood
Pinus strobus, white pine (aromatic)
Prunus spp., wild plums and cherries
Ptelea trifoliata, hop tree
Robinia pseudoacacia, black locust
Sassafras albidum, sassafras (aromatic)
Sorbus decora, showy mountain ash
Thuja occidentalis, arborvitae (aromatic)
Tilia americana, basswood
Viburnum lentago, nannyberry
Viburnum prunifolium, plum-leaved viburnum

Shrubs

Aesculus parviflora, bottlebrush buckeye
Calycanthus floridus 'Athens,' Carolina allspice (fragrant and aromatic)
Ceanothus americanus, New Jersey tea
Cephalanthus occidentalis, buttonbush

Clethra acuminata, cinnamon clethra

Clethra alnifolia, sweet pepperbush

Comptonia peregrina, sweetfern (aromatic)

Cornus alternifolia, pagoda dogwood

Fothergilla gardenii, dwarf fothergilla (fragrant and aromatic)

Fothergilla major, fothergilla

Hamamelis vernalis, vernal witch hazel (fragrant and aromatic)

Hamamelis virginiana, witch hazel (fragrant and aromatic)

Ilex glabra, inkberry

Itea virginica, sweetspire (fragrant and aromatic)

Juniperus spp., creeping junipers (aromatic)

Ledum groenlandicum, Labrador tea (aromatic)

Lindera benzoin, spicebush (both)

Lonicera canadensis, fly honeysuckle

Myrica (*Morella*) *pensylvanica*, bayberry (aromatic)

Physocarpus opulifolia, common ninebark

Pieris floribunda, mountain pieris

Rhododendron spp. (*alabamense, arborescens, atlanticum, austrinum,*
    canescens, periclymenoides, prinophyllum, and *viscosum*), wild azaleas

Rhus aromatica, fragrant sumac (aromatic)

Rosa palustris, swamp rose

Rosa virginiana, Virginia rose

Rubus odoratus, fragrant thimbleberry

Sambucus canadensis, elderberry

Sambucus pubens, red elder

Taxus candensis, Canada yew (aromatic)

Viburnum cassinoides, wild raisin

Vines

Apios americana, groundnut

Aristolochia durior, Dutchman's pipe (aromatic)

Gelsemium sempervirens, Carolina jessamine

Lonicera dioica, limber honeysuckle

Rosa setigera, climbing rose

Vitis spp., wild grapes

Wisteria macrostachya, Kentucky wisteria

Wildflowers

Asclepias quadrifolia, whorled milkweed

Asclepias syriaca, common milkweed

Epigaea repens, mayflower (fragrant and aromatic)

Gaultheria procumbens, wintergreen (aromatic)

Helonias bullata, swamp pink

Monarda spp., beebalms (aromatic)

Oenothera biennis, evening primrose

Phlox divaricata, woodland phlox

Phlox paniculata, garden phlox (older cultivars have stronger scent)

Pycnanthemum spp., mountain mint (aromatic)

Spiranthes odorata 'Chadd's Ford,' fragrant lady's tresses

Trillium luteum, yellow trillium (lemon-scented)

Trillium vaseyi, Vasey's trillium (rose-scented)

Yucca filamentosa, Adam's needle

Aquatics

Nymphaea odorata, fragrant water lily

Saururus cernuus, lizard's tail

K. INDIGENOUS ANNUALS AND BIENNIALS

Numerous species of indigenous plants complete their life cycles in either one (annual) or two (biennial) growing seasons. The ones included below represent only a small sample of some of the more common species.

Annuals

Bidens aristosa, tickseed sunflower
Bidens cernua, bur marigold
Bidens coronata, crowned tickseed
Campanulastrum americanum, tall bellflower
Cassia (*Chamaechrista*) *fasciculata*, partridge pea
Collinsia verna, blue-eyed Mary
Coreopsis tinctoria, golden tickseed
Cucurbita pepo var. *ovifera*, field pumpkin
Cucurbita pepo var. *ozarkana*, Ozark wild gourd
Diamorpha smallii, Small's stonecrop
Erigeron annuus, eastern daisy fleabane
Eustoma exaltatum subsp. *russellianum*, prairie gentian
Helianthus annuus, sunflower
Houstonia pusilla, annual bluet
Impatiens capensis, jewelweed
Monarda punctata, spotted beebalm
Nicotiana repanda, fiddleleaf tobacco
Phacelia maculata, spotted phacelia
Phacelia purshii, Miami mist
Phlox drummondii, annual phlox
Rudbeckia hirta, black-eyed Susan
Salvia azurea, azure blue sage
Salvia coccinea, scarlet sage
Verbena stricta, hoary vervain

Biennials

Adlumia fungosa, bleeding heart vine
Corydalis sempervirens, rock harlequin
Gaura biennis, biennial beeblossom
Ipomopsis rubra, standing cypress
Oenothera biennis, evening primrose
Phacelia bipinnatifida, fernleaf phacelia
Verbena hastata, blue vervain

L. SUGGESTED SOURCES OF INDIGENOUS PLANTS

The Internet has made plant shopping almost too easy. It is now possible to search for any plant by name, and sources from which to purchase it rise quickly to the top of the list. Below, some native plant and specialty nurseries are listed as a starting point.

Broken Arrow Nursery
13 Broken Arrow Rd.
Hamden, Conn. 06518
203-288-1026
http://www.brokenarrownursery.com
(Mountain laurels, plus many other native trees and shrubs)

Catskill Native Nursery
607 Samsonville Rd.
Kerhonkson, N.Y. 12446
845-626-2758
http://www.catskillnativenursery.com
(No mail order)

Environmental Concern
P.O. Box P
St. Michaels, Md. 21663
410-745-9620
http://www.wetland.org
(Wetland plants)

Ernst Conservation Seeds
9006 Mercer Pike
Meadville, Pa. 16335
800-873-3321
http://www.ernstseed.com
(Meadow seeds)

Musser Forests, Inc.
1880 Route 119 Hwy N
Indiana, Pa. 15701-7341
800-643-8319
http://www.musserforests.com
(Many native trees and shrubs)

Native Landscapes, Inc.
P.O. Box 327
Pawling, N.Y. 12564
845-855-7050
http://www.nativelandscaping.net
(No mail order)

New England Wild Flower Society
    Nasami Nursery
128 North St.
Whately, Mass. 01373
413-397-9922
http://www.newfs.org
(No mail order)

North Creek Nursery
388 North Creek Rd.
Landenburg, Pa. 19350
877-326-7584
http://www.northcreeknurseries.com
(Perennials, wholesale only)

Pinelands
323 Island Rd.
Columbus, N.J. 08022
609-291-9486
http://www.pinelandsnursery.com
(Wetland plants, wholesale only)

Pine Ridge Gardens
P.O. Box 200
London, Ark. 72847-0200
479-293-4359
http://www.pineridgegardens.com
(All native plants, many
northeastern)

Prairie Moon Nursery
32115 Prairie Lane
Winona, Minn. 55987
507-452-1362
http://www.prairiemoon.com
(Meadow seeds and plants)

Prairie Nursery
P.O. Box 306
Westfield, Wis. 53964
800-476-9453
http://www.prairienursery.com
(Meadow seeds and plants)

Rare Find Nursery
957 Patterson Rd.
Jackson, N.J. 08527
732-833-0613
http://www.rarefindnursery.com
(Rhododendrons and many other
species indigenous to the New
Jersey pinelands)

Shooting Star Nursery
444 Bates Rd.
Frankfort, Ky. 40601
502-223-1679
http://www.shootingstarnursery.com
(All native: perennials, trees, and
shrubs)

M. INDIGENOUS PLANTS COMMONLY SOLD IN NURSERIES

There is no need to search too far from home to find a source of indigenous plants. Many listed below can be found at local garden centers.

Trees
Acer ×freemanii, hybrid maple
Amelanchier ×grandiflora, hybrid juneberry
Betula nigra, river birch
Crateagus viridis 'Winter King,' green hawthorn
Oxydendron arboreum, sourwood
Picea glauca (dwarf cvs.), white spruce

Shrubs
Amelanchier canadensis, shadbush
Arctostaphylos uva-ursi (evergreen groundcover), bearberry
Aronia (*Photinia*) *arbutifolia* 'Brilliantissima,' red chokebery
Cornus alternifolia, pagoda dogwood
Hydrangea quercifolia, oak-leaved hydrangea
Ilex glabra, inkberry
Juniperus horizontalis (evergreen groundcover), creeping juniper
Potentilla fruticosa, shrubby cinquefoil
Sambucus canadensis, elderberry
Viburnum dentatum, arrowwood
Viburnum lentago, nannyberry
Viburnum opulus var. *americanum*, American cranberrybush
Viburnum prunifolium, plum-leaved viburnum

Wildflowers
Aster divaricatus, white wood aster
Aster laevis 'Bluebird,' smooth blue aster
Aster lateriflorus, calico aster
Aster novi-belgii, New York aster
Chrysogonum virginianum 'Allen Bush,' green and gold
Dicentra eximia, wild bleeding heart
Eupatorium fistulosum 'Atropurpureum,' Joe-Pye weed
Eupatorium maculatum 'Gateway,' spotted Joe-Pye weed

Eupatorium rugosum 'Chocolate,' white snakeroot
Heliopsis helianthoides, oxeye
Heuchera americana, alumroot
Heuchera villosa, hairy alumroot
Oenothera fruticosa, sundrops
Penstemon digitalis, beardtongue
Physostegia virginiana, obedient plant
Polemonium reptans, Jacob's ladder
Rudbeckia hirta, annual black-eyed Susan
Solidago rugosa 'Fireworks,' rough goldenrod
Viola labradorica, Labrador violet

Grasses and Sedges
Carex pensylvanica, Pennsylvania sedge
Panicum virgatum, panic grass
Schizachyrium scoparium, little bluestem
Sorghastrum nutans, Indian grass
Sporobolus heterolepis, prairie dropseed

Ferns
Athyrium filix-femina, lady fern
Dryopteris intermedia, common woodfern
Dryopteris marginalis, marginal woodfern
Onoclea sensibilis, sensitive fern
Polystichum acrostichoides, Christmas fern

BIBLIOGRAPHY

Adams, Denise Wiles. *Restoring American Gardens: An Encyclopedia of Heirloom Orna-mental Plants, 1640–1940.* Portland, Ore.: Timber Press, 2004.

Alien Plant Working Group. Weeds Gone Wild: Alien Plant Invaders of Natural Areas. http://www.nps.gov/plants/ALIEN/index.htm.

American Bird Conservancy. Cats Indoors! The Campaign for Safer Birds and Cats. http://www.abcbirds.org/abcprograms/policy/cats/index.html.

Armitage, Allan M. *Armitage's Native Plants for North American Gardens.* Portland, Ore.: Timber Press, 2006.

Barrington, David S., and Catherine A. Parris. "Refugia and Migration in the Quater-nary History of the New England Flora." *Rhodora* 109(940) (2007): 369–386.

Baskin, Yvonne. "Nature's Space Invaders." *Nature Conservancy Newsletter* (Summer 2002).

———. *A Plague of Rats and Rubbervines: The Growing Threat of Species Invasions.* Washington, D.C.: Shearwater Books/Island Press, 2002.

Bertin, Robert I., Megan E. Manner, Brian F. Larrow, Timothy W. Cantwell, and Eliz-abeth M. Berstene. "Norway Maple (*Acer platanoides*) and Other Non-native Trees in Urban Woodlands of Central Massachusetts." *Journal of the Torrey Botanical Society* 132(2) (2005): 225–235.

Borgmann, Kathi L., and Amanda D. Rodewald. "Nest Predation in an Urbanizing Landscape: The Role of Exotic Shrubs." *Ecological Applications* 14(6) (2004): 1,757–1,765.

Bowen, Beverly Z. "Pipe-Dreams Can Come True." *Butterfly Gardener* 10 (2005): 8–9.

Bowers, Clement Gray. *Rhododendrons and Azaleas: Their Origins, Cultivation and Development.* New York: Macmillan, 1936.

Bowers, Michael. "Bumble Bee Colonization, Extinction, and Reproduction in Sub-alpine Meadows in Northwestern Utah." *Ecology* 66(3) (1985): 914–927.

Buchmann, Stephen L., and Gary P. Nabhan. *The Forgotten Pollinators.* Washington, D.C.: Island Press, 1997.

Burrell, C. Colston. *A Gardener's Encyclopedia of Wildflowers: An Organic Guide to Choos-ing and Growing over 150 Beautiful Wildflowers.* Emmaus, Pa.: Rodale Press, 1997.

———. *Native Alternatives to Invasive Plants.* New York: Brooklyn Botanic Garden, 2006.

Caillet, Marie, et al., contrib. eds. *The Louisiana Iris: The Taming of a Native American Wildflower.* 2nd ed. Portland, Ore.: Timber Press, 2000.

Center for Plant Conservation. http://www.centerforplantconservation.org.

Clements, Steven, and Carol Gracie. *Wildflowers in the Field and Forest: A Field Guide to the Northeastern United States.* New York: Oxford University Press, 2006.

Connecticut Botanical Society. http://www.ct-botanical-society.org/index.html.

Cooper, Guy, Gordon Taylor, and Clive Boursnell. *English Herb Gardens.* New York: Rizzoli International Publications, 1986.

Cornell Lab of Ornithology. http://www.birds.cornell.edu.

Cullina, William. *Native Ferns, Moss and Grasses.* Boston: Houghton Mifflin, 2008.

――――. *Native Trees, Shrubs, and Vines: A Guide to Using, Growing, and Propagating North American Woody Plants.* Boston: Houghton Mifflin, 2002.

――――. *The New England Wild Flower Society Guide to Growing and Propagating Wildflowers of the United States and Canada.* Boston: Houghton Mifflin, 2000.

Dickinson, M. B., *Field Guide to the Birds of North America.* 3rd ed. Washington, D.C.: National Geographic Society, 1999.

Dirr, Michael A. *Viburnums: Flowering Shrubs for Every Season.* Portland, Ore.: Timber Press, 2007.

Dole, Claire Hagen, ed. *The Butterfly Gardener's Guide.* New York: Brooklyn Botanic Garden, 2003.

Driscoll, Carlos A., Juliet Clutton-Brock, Andrew C. Kitchener, and Stephen J. O'Brien. "The Taming of the Cat." *Scientific American,* June 2009, 68–75.

Ehrenfeld, Joan G. "Invasion of Deciduous Forest Preserves in the New York Metropolitan Region by Japanese Barberry (*Berberis thunbergii* DC.)." *Journal of the Torrey Botanical Society* 124 (1999): 210–215.

Fabbro, Cece. "Ephemeral Beauty." *Wildflower* (Lady Bird Johnson Wildflower Center) 2(3) (2007): 21–27.

Fine Gardening. July/August 2008.

Gargiullo, Margaret B. *A Guide to the Native Plants of the New York City Region.* New Brunswick, N.J.: Rutgers University Press, 2007.

Gill, John Freeman. "Keeping Tabs on Feathered Waistlines." *New York Times,* May 8, 2005.

Gilliam, Frank S., and Mark R. Roberts, eds. *The Herbaceous Layer in Forests of Eastern North America.* New York: Oxford University Press, 2003.

Gillman, Edward F. *Trees for Urban and Suburban Landscapes.* Albany, N.Y.: Delmar Publishers, 1997.

Gleason, Henry A., and Arthur Cronquist. *Manual of Vascular Plants of Northeastern United States and Adjacent Canada.* Bronx, N.Y.: New York Botanical Garden, 1991.

Hatfield, Richard G., and Gretchen LeBuhn. "Patch and Landscape Factors Shape Community Assemblage of Bumble Bees, *Bombus* spp. (Hymenoptera: Apidae), in Montane Meadows." *Biological Conservation* 139 (1–2) (2007): 150–158.

Heims, Dan, and Grahame Ware. *Heucheras and Heucherellas*. Portland, Ore.: Timber Press, 2005.

Hightshoe, Gary L. *Native Trees, Shrubs, and Vines for Urban and Rural America: A Planting Design Manual for Environmental Designers*. New York: Van Nostrand Rheinhold, 1988.

Holmes, Richard T., and Thomas W. Sherry. "Thirty-Year Bird Population Trends in an Unfragmented Temperate Deciduous Forest: Importance of Habitat Change." *Auk* 118(3) (2001): 589–609.

Hudak, Joseph. *Gardening with Perennials Month by Month*. 2nd ed. Portland, Ore.: Timber Press, 1993.

Jackson, Bernard, and Valerie Baines. *Mindful of Butterflies*. Sussex, U.K.: Book Guild, 1999.

Jaynes, Richard A. *Kalmia: The Laurel Book II*. Portland, Ore.: Timber Press, 1988.

Jekyll, Gertrude. *Wall and Water Gardens*. 1901. Rev. 1983 by Graham Stuart Thomas. Salem, N.H.: Ayer Co.

Johnson, Robert A., Mary F. Willson, John Thompson, and Robert I. Bertin. "Nutritional Values of Wild Fruits and Consumption by Migrant Frugivorous Birds." *Ecology* 66(3) (1985): appendix.

Jones, Jason, Patrick J. Doran, and Richard T. Holmes. "Climate and Food Synchronize Regional Forest Bird Abundances." *Ecology* 84(11) (2003): 3,024–3,032.

Killmaster, Charles H., David A. Osborne, Robert J. Warren, and Karl V. Miller. "Deer and Understory Plant Responses to a Large-Scale Herd Reduction on a Georgia State Park." *Natural Areas Journal* 27 (2007):161–168.

Kolbert, Elizabeth. "Turf War." *New Yorker*, July 21, 2008.

Kress, Stephen W. *The Audubon Society Guide to Attracting Birds*. 2nd ed. Ithaca, N.Y.: Cornell University Press, 2006.

Lady Bird Johnson Wildflower Center. Native Plant Information Network. http://www.wildflower.org.

Leopold, Donald J. *Native Plants of the Northeast: A Guide for Gardening and Conservation*. Portland, Ore.: Timber Press, 2005.

Love, Jason P. "Effects of Morrow's Honeysuckle Control and the Impact of the Shrub on Invertebrates at Fort Necessity National Battlefield, Pennsylvania." Master's thesis, Davis College of Agriculture, Forestry, and Consumer Sciences at West Virginia University, 2006.

Mann, Charles C. "America, Found and Lost," *National Geographic*, May 2007.

Marinelli, Janet. *Stalking the Wild Amaranth: Gardening in the Age of Extinction*. New York: Henry Holt, 1998.

———. *The Wildlife Gardener's Guide*. New York: Brooklyn Botanic Garden, 2008.

Martin, Alexander C., Herbert S. Zim, and Arnold L. Nelson. *American Wildlife and Plants: A Guide to Wildlife Food Habits*. 1951. Reprint, New York: Dover, 1961.

Martin, Tovah, ed. *Old-Fashioned Flowers: Classic Blossoms to Grow in Your Garden*. New York: Brooklyn Botanic Garden, 2000.

McGary, Jane, ed. *Rock Garden Plants of North America*. Portland, Ore.: Timber Press, 1996.

McHarg, Ian L. *Design with Nature*. Garden City, N.Y.: Natural History Press, 1969.

McShea, William J., and John Rappole. "Managing the Abundance and Diversity of Breeding Bird Populations through Manipulation of Deer Populations." *Conservation Biology* 14(4) (2000): 1,161–1,170.

Minckley, Robert L., J. H. Cane, and L. Kervin. "Origins and Ecological Consequences of Pollen Specialization among Desert Bees." *Proceedings of the Royal Society of London* B 267 (2000): 265–271.

Mitchell, Richard S. *A Checklist of New York State Plants*. Bulletin no. 458. Albany: New York State Museum, the University of the State of New York, 1986.

National Wildlife Federation Backyard Wildlife Habitat Certification. http://.nwf.org/backyard.

Native Plant Center at Westchester Community College. http://www.nativeplantcenter.org.

Newcomb, Lawrence. *Newcomb's Wildflower Guide*. Boston: Little, Brown, 1977.

Opler, Paul, and George O. Krizek. *Butterflies East of the Great Plains: An Illustrated Natural History*. Baltimore: Johns Hopkins University Press, 1984.

Opler, Paul A., Kelly Lotts, and Thomas Naberhaus, coordinators. Butterflies and Moths of North America. Bozeman, Mont.: Big Sky Institute. http://www.butterfliesandmoths.org.

Ostfeld, Richard S. "The Ecology of Lyme-Disease Risk." *American Scientist* 85 (1997): 338–346.

Palm, Mary E. "Systematics and the Impact of Invasive Fungi on Agriculture in the United States." *BioScience* 51(2) (2001): 141–147.

Pellett, Frank C. *Flowers of the Wild*. New York: A. T. DeLaMare Co., 1931.

Picton, Paul. *The Gardener's Guide to Growing Asters*. Portland, Ore.: Timber Press, 1999.

Preston, Richard. "A Death in the Forest." *New Yorker*, December 10, 2007.

Pyle, Robert M. *Handbook for Butterfly Watchers*. Boston: Houghton Mifflin, 1984.

Randall, John M., and Janet Marinelli, eds. *Invasive Plants: Weeds of the Global Garden*. New York: Brooklyn Botanic Garden, 1996.

Rawinski, Thomas J. "Impacts of White-Tailed Deer Overabundance in Forest Ecosystems: An Overview." Washington, D.C.: Forest Service, U.S. Department of Agriculture, 2008.

Reschke, Carol. *Ecological Communities of New York State*. New York Natural Heritage Program. Latham, N.Y.: New York State Department of Environmental Conservation, 1990.

Roberts, Edith A., and Elsa Rehmann. *American Plants for American Gardeners*. 1929. Reprint, with foreword by Darrel G. Morrison, Athens: University of Georgia Press, 1996.

Robinson, G. S., et al. HOSTS—a Database of the World's Lepidopteran Hostplants. http://www.nhm.ac.uk/research-curation/research/projects/hostplants.

Rossell, C. Reed, Jr., Steven Patch, and Susan Salmons. "Effects of Deer Browsing on Native and Non-native Vegetation in a Mixed Oak-Beech Forest on the Atlantic Coastal Plain." *Northeastern Naturalist* 14(1) (2007): 61–72.

Rothschild, Miriam. "What Do Butterflies See?" 1983. Reprinted in Xerces Society/Smithsonian Institution, *Butterfly Gardening: Creating Summer Magic in Your Garden*. San Francisco: Sierra Club Books, 1990.

Sauer, Leslie J., and Andropogon Associates. *The Once and Future Forest: A Guide to Forest Restoration Strategies.* Washington, D.C.: Island Press, 1998.

Schmidt, Kenneth A., and Christopher J. Whelan. "Effects of *Lonicera* and *Rhamnus* on Songbird Nest Predation." *Conservation Biology* 13(6) (1999): 1,502–1,506.

Shepard, Matthew, Steven L. Buchmann, Marc Vaughn, and Scott Hoffman Black. *Pollinator Conservation Handbook.* Portland, Ore.: Xerces Society, in association with Bee Works, 2003.

Slawson, David. "Authenticity in the Japanese Garden." In *Japanese-Inspired Gardens*, 21st Century Gardening Series, Janet Marinelli, series ed., Patricia Jonas, guest ed. New York: Brooklyn Botanic Garden, 2001.

Smith, Julian. "How North American Agriculture Began." *American Archeology* 12(1) (2008): 19–26.

Smith, Susan B., Kathleen McPherson, Jeffrey M. Backer, Barbara J. Pierce, David Polesak, and Scott R. McWilliams. "Fruit Quality and Consumption by Songbirds during Autumn Migration." *Wilson Journal of Ornithology* 119(3) (2007): 419–428.

Stein, Sara. *Noah's Garden: Restoring the Ecology of Our Own Back Yards.* New York: Houghton Mifflin, 1993.

Sternberg, Guy, with Jim Wilson. *Native Trees for North American Landscapes.* Portland, Ore.: Timber Press, 2004.

Stinson, K. A., S. A. Campbell, J. R. Powell, B. E. Wolfe, R. M. Callaway, et al. "Invasive Plant Suppresses the Growth of Native Tree Seedlings by Disrupting Belowground Mutualisms." *PLoS Biology* 4(5) (2006): 0727–0731. Available at http://www.plosbiology.org.

Sumner, Judith. *American Household Botany: A History of Useful Plants, 1620–1900.* Portland, Ore.: Timber Press, 2004.

Tallamy, Douglas W. *Bringing Nature Home: How Native Plants Sustain Wildlife in Our Gardens.* Portland, Ore.: Timber Press, 2007.

———. "Do Alien Plants Reduce Insect Biomass?" *Conservation Biology* 18(6) (2004): 1,689–1,692.

———. Tallamy home page, University of Delaware. http://copland.udel.edu/~dtallamy.

Towe, L. C. *American Azaleas.* Portland, Ore.: Timber Press, 2004.

USDA NRCS. The PLANTS Database. National Plant Data Center, Baton Rouge, La. http://plants.usda.gov.

Utz, Ryan M. "Temporal Trends in Consumption, Growth, and Successful Feeding Traits of a Central Appalachian Brook Trout Population at the Watershed Scale." Master's thesis, Davis College of Agriculture, Forestry, and Consumer Sciences, West Virginia University, 2005.

Vickery, Peter D., and Peter W. Dunwiddie, eds. *Grasslands of Northeastern North America: Ecology and Conservation of Native and Agricultural Landscapes.* Lincoln: Massachusetts Audubon Society, 1997.

Wagner, David L. *Caterpillars of Eastern North America.* Princeton, N.J.: Princeton University Press, 2005.

Williams, Neal M., and Claire Kreman. "Resource Distributions among Habitats Determine Solitary Bee Offspring Production in a Mosaic Landscape." *Ecological Applications* 17(3) (2007): 910–921.

Williams, Scott C., Jeffrey S. Ward, Thomas E. Worthley, and Kirby C. Stafford. "Managing Japanese Barberry Infestations Reduces Blacklegged Tick (Acari: Ixodidae) Abundances." Connecticut Agricultural Experiment Station, New Haven, Conn., draft submitted for publication.

Wilson, E. O. "The Little Things That Run the World (the Importance and Conservation of Invertebrates)." *Conservation Biology* 1(4) (1987): 344–346.

Wilson, Mark V., Paul C. Hammond, and Cheryl B. Schultz. "The Interdependence of Native Plants and Fender's Blue Butterfly." In *Conservation and Management of Native Flora and Fungi*, ed. T. N. Kaye et al., 83–87. Corvallis: Native Plant Society of Oregon, 1997.

Yahner, Richard H. "Butterfly Communities in Residential Landscapes of Central Pennsylvania." *Northeastern Naturalist* 8(1) (2001): 113–118.

INDEX

Page numbers in italics indicate illustrations.

ABOUT THE AUTHOR

Carolyn Summers is an adjunct professor for continuing education at Westchester Community College and provides technical assistance to the Native Plant Center there, an affiliate of the Ladybird Johnson Wildflower Center. She created and maintains two demonstration gardens that display indigenous plants, one at her family's suburban home and the other at their three-hundred-acre Flying Trillium Arboretum. She received her degree in landscape architecture from City College of New York and has more than fifteen years of experience in the environmental and landscape design field, working for nonprofit and government agencies, including the New York City Department of Environmental Protection (NYCDEP), the Natural Resources Defense Council, and the Trust for Public Land. Projects have ranged widely, from designing an urban wildlife refuge to building a watershed forestry coalition to producing a comprehensive report analyzing and critiquing the environmental programs of the New York–New Jersey metropolitan region. Of particular relevance to this book, while at NYCDEP, she researched and implemented a "plant indigenous only" policy, which continues in effect, for New York City's environmental construction projects.